BEST CANADIAN POETRY
2023

BEST
CANADIAN
POETRY

2023

GUEST EDITOR: JOHN BARTON

SERIES EDITOR: ANITA LAHEY

BIBLIOASIS

WINDSOR, ONTARIO

FIRST EDITION

ISBN 978-1-77196-499-9 (Trade Paper)
ISBN 978-1-77196-500-2 (eBook)

Series editor: Anita Lahey
Guest editor: John Barton
Editors at Large: Michael Fraser, Laboni Islam, waaseyaa'sin christine sy
Copyeditor: John Sweet
Cover and text design: Gordon Robertson

Published with the generous assistance of the Canada Council for the Arts,
which last year invested $153 million to bring the arts to Canadians throughout
the country, and the financial support of the Government of Canada. Biblioasis
also acknowledges the support of the Ontario Arts Council (OAC), an agency
of the Government of Ontario, which last year funded 1,709 individual artists
and 1,078 organizations in 204 communities across Ontario, for a total of
$52.1 million, and the contribution of the Government of Ontario through the
Ontario Book Publishing Tax Credit and Ontario Creates.

PRINTED AND BOUND IN CANADA

CONTENTS

FOREWORD

Poems for "just ones" and "approximate beings"

> Just read the work and love whatever feels alive, whatever jolts you into new frames of feeling and thought.
>
> — Steven Heighton,
> *Workbook: memos and dispatches on writing*

As I write this foreword for the fifteenth edition of *Best Canadian Poetry,* poets and others in the community of writers and readers are mourning the loss of Kingston author Steven Heighton. I, like many, have sought solace in the words he left us, especially those he strung masterfully, delicately, into poems. As I read, the lines unfold in my mind in the low, gentle register of his voice. They are, I have noticed afresh, peopled with ghosts—friends and family and others who came to reside within the arc of his keen, generous attention. I turn to his poem "Christmas Work Detail, Samos," drawn from his experiences working among volunteers and Syrian refugees in Greece in 2015. This composition of almost unbearably formal quatrains—unbearable for the anguish, rage, and humanity they encapsulate—imparts an ongoing tragedy in a resonant, rhythmic, near-Biblical voice:

> In the olive grove on the high ground, facing west
> into rain, we dig graves for three men drowned
> in the straits—Syrians, maybe, dispossessed
> of everything by the sea, so there's no knowing

How does a poet access the language necessary to usher the reader into the heart of such a scene, and into the grim reality that caused it? In *Workbook,* from which the epigraph above is taken, Heighton defines poetry as "the art of calling things by their true and secret name." He knew better than anyone the oft-seeming futility of such a task, how elusive the right words, the necessary and called-for words—or, conversely, how inadequate the available words—can seem. And yet how crucial.

Heighton's poem "Some Other Just Ones," written "after Borges," was first published in *The Walrus* and appeared in *Best Canadian Poetry 2010.* In 2017, it was selected by myself and Molly Peacock, this anthology's original series editor, for *The Best of the Best Canadian Poetry.* Sue Goyette, *BCP*'s 2010 guest editor, noted Heighton's "just ones" in her introduction, particularly those "who redeem from neglect a gorgeous, long-orphaned word." Questions arise. Why was this word widely forgotten? What difference will it make to the person in whose mouth it's resurrected? To the one in whose ear it lands, after this long period of dormancy and silence? Goyette quotes Albert Camus, who charged (in a way, condemning us all) that, "Naming an object inaccurately means adding to the unhappiness of the world." But to do the work of Heighton's "just ones" and bring back a lost word—then to use it precisely where it's required—would surely accomplish the opposite: it would *add* to the happiness of the world. It would insert a discernible notch between our position and that of despair. To slot the word in its rightful place, then speak it aloud, would suspend us—in a world where every second counts—just that little bit longer above the mire.

Implicit in Heighton's behest that we "just read the work and love whatever feels alive" is the belief that language breathes and moves. *Just read the work and love* ... It's a plea, infused with Heighton's characteristic urgency, for us to slip outside aesthetic territories, eschew superficial performance, and let ourselves travel to the very real places from which the words come, and to where they lead. *Just read the work and love* ... It's both imperative and permission. It's what we ask of this anthology's guest editor each year as they pour through the thousand-plus poems we pass on to them from the previous year's journals. It's also what we ask of the reader who picks up this volume containing the fifty poems that editor most loved, the ones that, for them, came most forcefully alive.

*

I have come to recognize that each poem is a wild animal
at liberty somewhere in nature ...

— John Barton, from the essay "Inside the Blind: On
Editing Poetry," in the collection *We Are Not Avatars*

When we recruit guest editors for *Best Canadian Poetry*, we seek out people who engage with the craft beyond the confines of their own work, whether that be through a practice of reviewing, of editing, of teaching and mentoring, or other acts of literary reciprocity. We want editors who are willing—even better, compelled—to contribute to our understanding of poetry past and present, including how today's Canadian poets are tasting, testing, relishing, and remixing this most potent of literary disciplines. We want people who've demonstrated humility in the face of the craft, who have struggled to isolate its ingredients, who show judicious respect for its effects.

This year's guest editor, John Barton, might well represent the gold standard for heightened literary engagement, and for exhibiting a healthy deference toward poetry's wiles—while likewise showing no hesitation to use them for his own ends. John has mentored emerging poets; edited and consulted on a long line of manuscripts; lectured on poetry and on poetry editing; held writer-in-residence positions across the country; nurtured a generation of reviewers; written in-depth essays on the works of a storied list of poets that includes Margaret Avison, Billy-Ray Belcourt, Anne Szumigalski, and Ben Ladouceur; co-edited the groundbreaking *Seminal: The Anthology of Canada's Gay-Male Poets;* and finally, put in thirty years editing literary journals, first *Arc Poetry Magazine* and then *The Malahat Review*.

Barton has played such a profound and influential role as an editor and mentor over the past few decades—and, not insignificantly, as a skilful navigator (and, as you'll see in his introductory essay, analyst) of the labyrinthine funding landscape in which Canlit resides—that his own work risks being overshadowed. This ought not to be the case. Barton is one of this country's most adventurous and sophisticated poets, his output unbroken over four-plus decades, his voice unmistakable. His work is notably and consistently brave. Like the subject of Michael Dunwoody's poem in this anthology, "The Last Thing I'll Remember"—"who published / him/him poems before it was the thing"—Barton was publishing openly gay poetry in Canada before such content was either common or widely welcomed. Decades ago he wrote poems that challenged gender norms while transcending the limits of any particular identity, whether imposed, newly found, rehabilitated, or reclaimed. His extraordinary book-length poem *Hidden Structure,* written when he was twenty-one and published in 1984, wrestles with sexuality in tight lines and with searing honesty. "Something is missing," he writes. "We are all approximate beings / made proximate by love." And later, "for once I know / what I am trying to say. / Those who love shall love / no matter how the bodies join." R.M. Vaughan wrote, in his introduction to *The Boy with the Eyes of the Virgin,* Barton's 2012 selected poems (we are long overdue for an update of this valuable volume): "John Barton is the most alert poet I know. He misses nothing, his poetry even less. Read a John Barton poem and find a world encapsulated, held close, closer than a lover, but never asphyxiated. John's poems breathe, pulse, occasionally bark, and always, always bite. They do this because they no longer fear to be; a man or whatever's going around."

They no longer fear to be. Barton's is a poetry of realization: of facing one's monsters, one's most daunting or most frighteningly enticing questions, and becoming the person on the other side of that blood-curdling but necessary—and necessarily invigorating—encounter. We're talking transformation. We're talking the stuff of myth.

Many years ago, while touring classes of high school English students through the National Gallery of Canada (and leading them in writing exercises prompted by artworks), I often shared Barton's poem "Autumn in France," inspired by the Emily Carr painting of the same name that was on display in the Canadian galleries. The poem begins with a harsh, self-imposed judgment: "My eyes shrink from this canvas, / my attempt at light. / Was I blind // to what I saw then?" I explained that the poem was from Barton's collection *West of Darkness,* a "portrait in verse" of Carr, in which he takes on her voice—rather, his imagined version of her voice, which, by virtue of the way such creativity works, then functions as a kind of instrument or container for his own voice, or a version of it, newly tried on or changed.

One day, while we were discussing "Autumn in France," a student objected. What right had Barton, a man, to adopt Carr's voice? In answer, I didn't declare that Barton did or did not have that "right." But I did speak of the honest toil of the imagination, and the integrity of that toil when informed by serious and extensive research and reflection. I spoke of the centuries-long history of ekphrasis, in which writers respond creatively to visual art and vice versa, a vibrant practice that runs through Barton's oeuvre. I spoke of the risk artists take in making their work public, and the permission inherent in that sharing. And I spoke of the "right" we all have to respond to any art with which we have a meaningful encounter.

Barton's intimate journey through Carr's world, through her writing and her art and his own reactions to both, gave him a portal to an altered form, and a narrative to explore that was distinct from his own, but that wasn't unrelated to his own—because, in fact, no human story, no matter how distinct, is wholly disconnected from any other. He was interrogating Carr's artistic journey, but also her experience as a woman in what we've often called "a man's world," especially when speaking of her era (Carr was born in 1871). It's no surprise that *West of Darkness* was written in the years straddling the six months Barton spent composing *Hidden Structure*. Both are telling (and early) examples of Barton's willingness to venture, again and again via his poems, into his own unknowns (or should I say *partly*knowns), and then—this is related to how Heighton leads us through an olive grove toward those volunteers grimly digging graves—to gently but unapologetically carry his reader along with him. In his four-plus decades of writing and publishing poetry, Barton has moved doggedly through difficult, uncomfortable ground, from the political to the personal, or the other way around, often weaving both together with a precision, elegance of style, and subtle (yet wicked) humour that belies the dangers he's tucked into his hypnotic lines like cleverly disguised explosives.

I think of the harrowing poem "Portal," from Barton's 2009 collection *Hymn,* in which one kind of bomb is front and centre, others far less overt: "*Drop the bombs,* I say, *drop the bombs,* stand inside the portal / with your mother and hold your breath . . ." I think of "Pushing Upstream," from *Sweet Ellipsis* (1998): "Below my window, men in boats / are blasting a way into the river, moving // up from the mouth, / slowly, charge by charge, / exploding the myth . . ." I think of "In Hospital Scrubs, A Machinist," from *Windsock,* his 2018 chapbook of pain-related poems: "You cut me open, scal-pel picking apart / Silky layers of fat made to bleed in light / expose deep waywardness of my viscera..."

For many years Barton has formed his poems of single sentences, never allowing readers a full pause, just that half breath afforded by a line break, the odd comma. This exercise in stamina (for reader and writer) enacts the themes of endur-ance and survival that permeate his work. The constraint allows him to seamlessly braid in complexities of emotion and perspective. Caught in the momentum of those relent-less sentences, his lines waver, circle back, or leave him (and his reader) dangling off the ends of what seem like hopelessly tangled strings. At long last, after knotting and unknotting, after flinging himself out time and again like a kite catching an updraft, darting and swerving, Barton drifts and comes softly to ground. He writes in "Lost Self," one of the early son-nets that make up his astonishing poetic memoir *Lost Family* (Véhicule, 2020):

> Above and looking down before I was
> Born, I saw myself looking back, the light
> So strong it couldn't be seen through, a light
> Striation of cumulus stretched across

Barton's illuminating introduction to this volume is a tour de force, a piece of literary analysis that peels apart, layer by layer, the creative enterprise that is Canadian poetry—from funding models; to journal-making; to the fluctuating influ-ence of worldly matters on writers' concerns; to the welcome rise of historically marginalized voices; to the poet in private, rearranging their gatherings of words. Amidst all that, he leaves no poem in this anthology unremarked upon, and offers due credit to the journals that first chose to bring them to their readers. When you read it, and the poems collected here, you might find, as I have, that when making his selections, Barton responded, above all, to the bravery embedded in a work. To poetry that exhibits breadth and skill, no question. To voice, music, muscle, metaphor—of course. But those poems that bring readers to places they might not have thought to go, places readers may not have been sufficiently curious about, or even aware of—or to places they've neglected or were actively avoiding—these are the poems that Barton has chosen to highlight and to share. Poems that, like Armand Garnet Ruffo's "Observed and Observing, That's Him," place you, "a shamble of a man," "On a ladder balancing / off a roof." Poems that, like K.R. Segriff's "The Grannies in Dew Dresses," embed you in "sheets of soil and in the gloaming" with our deceased elders. Or that, like Sarah Yi-Mei Tsiang's "Choice," place the sonograph of a fetus at seven weeks in your direct line of sight: "small smudge / in webbed light."

Beth Goobie writes, in "You Are Story," the final poem in this book, "Principalities and dominions resonate under the bed, / press their netherworld claims on the mind." As writer, and as reader, Barton will always oblige: he'll not only enter those principalities and dominions, he'll remain there for a time, patiently taking in their swirls of "netherworld claims." He would instill that willingness in us all.

Anita Lahey
Ottawa/unceded Algonquin, Anishinabek territory
May 2022

INTRODUCTION

Nation-State of the Arts:
Thoughts on Culture That These Fifty Poems
Have Made Me Think

Over 2021, as boxes of magazines arrived by mail, I walked, as is my habit, around James Bay in Victoria. My pre-Confederation neighbourhood lies behind the provincial legislature, just south of the downtown core, and my apartment is one block from the Dallas Road seawall. Eighteen years ago, when I moved in, I didn't think that I could see the Strait of Juan da Fuca from my fourth-floor balcony until one day I noticed a cruise ship floating in a blue I'd earlier assumed was simply air. At the end of the Odgen Point Breakwater, I keep taking pictures of the clouds that the wind chases in from the open Pacific along the spine of the Olympic Mountains, which stand above the strait in Washington. Those clouds have yet to exhaust my interest, and a few hang so low they're sometimes the fog I emerge from when stepping off the breakwater onto the solidity of Vancouver Island.

I've found taking pictures on my iPhone to be as compulsive as the reading and writing of poetry. It's a tendency that has served me well as I ploughed through issue after print issue published in 2021 by literary magazines from across the country while keeping up with new content posted with asynchronous degrees of regularity by online journals. Like the digital photos I like to crop, most of these magazines, regardless of their formats, have a distinctive, if not necessarily unique, take on the kinds of poetry they deem worthy of their readers' attention. I suspect, however, that most magazines' editors, if asked, couldn't articulate what precisely informed their choices; the poems, as they were encountered on their pages by the likes of me, had to do the work of articulation themselves. Their appeal depends on their innate materiality (an aural tactility, if you will), to which their authors gave flesh technically and thematically through the diction, images, line breaks, cadences, and even the rhymes they felt most adeptly shaped their poems' otherwise stealth infrastructures. By publishing what they have, magazine editors have alleged, if not asserted, that these poems must or should compel our attention. At minimum, we should take a look, and look is what I have done, again and again and again.

So I need to come clean about something: while the co-editor of *Arc* and the editor of *The Malahat Review* (consecutive positions I occupied from 1988 to 2018), I hardly ever read any issue published by a "rival journal" from cover to cover—even when my own poems appeared in them, I'm embarrassed to say—as exhaustively as I have over the past year. I'd have argued in my defence that I'd already given almost all of my attention at the office—which I truly had, having likely read tens of thousands of pages of weak, mediocre, and promising writing in manuscript during my thirty-year-long, myopia-inducing career as a magazine editor. I'd joke that reading bad poetry ruined my nose for good (or had given me a guilty taste for bad poetry)—but that's of course not true, for excellent poems snapped me out of my ennui, their vitalizing perspectives rubbing the sleep out of my eyes. My goal was always to be jostled awake, and I soon realized that I was being jostled awake for two—myself and the reader.

Over the years, I'd choose poems less and less for myself and more and more for the people kind enough to read the two magazines I edited. I came to understand that my job description included an obligation to expose readers to wide varieties of poetry, to challenge their assumptions while expanding their taste. When readers said they loved everything in an issue, I'd be pleased, but secretly feel that I'd failed. If their experience of what they read was more mixed—they liked these poems or those poems but not the rest—I'd feel that I'd lived up to my responsibilities because if one reader was partial to one poem, a different reader would probably favour another. They may not have loved every poem (or, in the case of the *Malahat,* also every short story or essay) laid out for them, but I still hoped they'd give them each a first, a second, and even a third try, every time reflecting upon their growing appreciation or increasing revulsion. I hypothesized that their cumulative and contrary engagement could mean that *Arc*'s and the *Malahat*'s audiences were much bigger than if their editorial boards had not shown interest, however unwillingly, in many kinds of poetry and, if I was right, this could translate into larger, more diverse audiences for their contributors as well. It's in this same optimistic spirit that I have approached my role as guest editor for this edition of *Best Canadian Poetry*.

Now that I've read a reasonably representative sample of the magazine verse published in English by Canadian poets in 2021, I can say with gratitude that the endeavour has been worthwhile. My experience, if not my relief, as a reader cannot be too different from that of the jurors the Canada Council asks to evaluate the applications that arts and literary magazines submit to finagle some degree of financial support. Unlike those overworked jurors, I luckily wasn't obliged to assess how well candidate magazines adhere to the guidelines the Council expects them to follow in the fulfillment of its own agenda, one that, however putatively arm's-length, must fall somewhat in line with the government's own thinking about the arts—that is, when it's thinking about the arts—however much the intentions of both may deviate from the aspirations of the contributors appearing in the magazines they fund. Though in my role as guest editor I've been asked only to weigh the merits of the poetry they've published as poetry, I can't help also appreciating how adroitly the magazines have shot the rapids of government policy in an effort to reach "the silver reaches of the estuary" (to quote Margaret Avison) with a waterproof vision of what they each believe contemporary Canadian writing to be—all while somehow also staying afloat. Having submitted over thirty years' worth of applications to funders, I know a change can emerge out of nowhere in a peaceful stretch of previously paddled policy, one sharp and unprepared-for enough to make the possibility of sinking this time real. Not to go under—let alone lose all sense of where the silver reaches truly lie—is an achievement for which all the magazines I've read this year should be commended.

I used to believe that Canadian literary magazines were very much alike in what and who they published, but the reading I have done for *BCP* has shown me differently. The terrain upon which the magazines have optimistically set up shop seems to have experienced a few shifts in focus in the four years since January 2018, when I stepped down as the editor of *The Malahat Review*. These shifts warrant being mapped out, however shakily, before I move on to talk about the fifty poems you're about to read in depth. After all, they've reshaped the magazines that published them; editors may have been spurred to make decisions about what to publish in response. The poets have benefited, but has our appreciation of their poems increased?

What's most clearly evident is that the diversity that once, despite every best effort, seemed to elude many magazines has at long last made inroads into their pages. This is due in part to a new generation now leading them and in part because their editorial boards are themselves more diverse. I can only hope writers of many backgrounds submitting to them today do so with more faith that their work will be read with comprehension as well as empathy. The Canada Council has helped create the conditions for this: since 2017, it has tied sustained funding to increased space for Indigenous, racialized, and deaf and disabled voices. Another sign of change can be read in the contributor notes at the back of most magazines. Some readers perusing them may no longer recognize the country in which the writers indicate they reside; it's also possible that they may not realize they live there themselves. Instead of citing the geographical designations settlers have thumbtacked to the map—as I did to flag where I was from when I began publishing my poems in magazines in the late 1970s—contributors more often than not solely acknowledge the First Nations upon whose land they find themselves living as uninvited guests. As an arguably generous bone thrown to the confused, some put the settler name for where they are squatting in parentheses after its Indigenous name, or else they expect the reader to suss out where they live from the Indigenous spelling they have adopted for a place name that had been anglicized during colonization. The cynical may wonder to what degree some contributors are indulging in virtue signalling through their thumbnail autobiographies, but I enjoy being asked to acknowledge the larger story behind the dissembling overlay of my forebears, which the lands where I live (and have lived) continue to hold in trust and which Indigenous peoples have not forgotten. The disorientation is diverting, edifying, and anchoring.

Another notable change—likely not disconnected from the changes discussed above—pertains to tone and attack. If I had to characterize the poetry of the first two decades of the twenty-first century in a phrase, based on my time at *Arc* and at the *Malahat,* it would have to be as "benign eloquence." By this I mean a poetry that aims not to disturb in its extremely fine articulations; its watery surfaces often reflect light of such brilliance that one forgets to see if there's anything of depth struggling for affect behind them. Of course, the great practitioners of this tendency achieved eloquence without being benign; only their less skilled imitators, who still haven't noticed that their readers long ago drowned in less than an inch of their overheated bathwater, continue to sink so low, however pleasing their words at first blush may be. Though their work is not absent from the pages of today's magazines, editors have begun to break their stranglehold on readers' attention. In any case, they could hold on only so long before they got a kind of aesthetic carpal tunnel syndrome. Thank god they have let go a little so other kinds of writing can breathe. However, the "validating rhetoric" of some of today's writing, which aims to usher hegemony to the curb, does not necessarily make for better reading. This tendency, which appears closely tied to identity politics and intersectionality—for which the Canada Council's changed policies have, with good reason, helped to create space—likewise has its exemplars and less accomplished imitators.

The impulse behind identity politics is not new. To think that it should be recognized as innovative is an insult to the countless marginalized writers of past decades and earlier generations who likewise aimed to articulate a subjectivity different from that of their more widely published white, straight, male, and cis-gendered peers. These writers did not necessarily conceptualize their work as expressing positions characteristic of identity politics. "Politics" may not have been what they saw themselves as articulating; arguing that the personal is political was as far as some of us were prepared to go. Nor did they necessarily come to a better understanding of themselves by consciously looking through the prism of intersectionality, even if their life experience may have broken its light that way. Instead, their successes, failures, and unique ways of seeing prepared the ground for changes to come, and the Canada Council and the artistic community it aids and abets has begun to catch up. Some practitioners of validating rhetoric, however, share at least one misstep with those whose work evinces benign eloquence's most milquetoast tendencies: oversimplification.

As a queer poet, I feel that I have been "doing" some lonely form of identity politics for forty years while, at the same time, suffering the mainstream's reluctance to hear what I have had to say, especially in the early years. Today it's heartening to feel the comforting presence of other poets writing from their own versions of that lonely place as they have come to stand in increasing numbers around me—well, if not around me, then alongside those writers giving voice to experiences similar to theirs while advocating for "space" of their own in the zeitgeist (not a "room" like Virginia Woolf's, with something that passes for a view). In their poems, I recognize many strategies I've used to bring my own experiences forward, to speak through them for others like me, and to claim for them as well as for myself the reader's empathetic ear. There's a straightforwardness and forthrightness to these poems. By speaking plainly, their authors clearly don't wish to disappear behind the subterfuge that metaphor inevitably creates. What in other poets' hands would have been subtext rises to the surface as text: surface becomes depth, for what it speaks to without any apparent filters clearly is bottomless, if not fathomless.

Some magazines like *Contemporary Verse 2, PRISM international,* and *Room* appear more allied to identity politics and validating rhetoric; others like *The New Quarterly, Prairie Fire,* and, to a degree, *The Fiddlehead* tend not to wear their allegiances so obviously on their sleeves and also make room for poets less invested in identity politics or whose identities are so well in place that they believe the associated politics are so fully incorporated into their approach that it shapes what they have to say on any subject without straying too far into the reader's personal space. Magazines like *Arc* seem to be mapping a territory somewhere in between. This growing divergence in editorial approach has made Canada's literary magazine landscape far more interesting than it was.

Five superb theme issues published in the past year deserve singling out. Guest-edited by Ali Blythe and Trish Salal, *Arc*'s Spring 2021 issue, "Polymorphous *per* Verse," showcases trans, Two-Spirit, gender-nonconforming, and non-binary poetries (represented here by River Halen's "The Enemy"). "The Islands of Influence," *Arc*'s Fall 2021 issue guest-edited by Brandon Wint, explores the impact of Caribbean culture on North American poetry. "2S + QTBIPOC," *Contemporary Verse 2*'s Winter 2021 issue, delighted me more than any other issue. As guest editor Joshua Whitehead writes in his introduction, "its poems and [its] contributors highlight the vivacity and the tenacity of the BIPOC and queer voice" (represented here by Lucas Crawford's "Pet Names"). Similarly, *CV2*'s Summer 2021 issue, "Black Alive and Looking Back at You," guest-edited by Chimwemwe Undi and Leslie Joy Ahenda, "honour[s] the legacy of Black poetics that centres and celebrates the gifts of Black life, living and looking." Lastly, *Room*'s "Indigenous Brilliance" issue expands the definition of Indigeneity to include "every Black, Indigenous, and Afro-Indigenous creative" so that readers may be put "in conversation with global indigeneity and global entanglements of colonialism and imperialism." For this issue, *Room* collective members Karmella Cen Benedito De Barros, Jessica Johns, Patricia Massy, Emily Dundas Oke, and jaye simpson consciously assembled "voices varied in where they come from and the experiences they speak" (represented here by Samantha Nock's "kiskatinaw interlude" and Michelle Porter's "Parts of the Needle, Manitoba, Canada 1870").

All but one of these five issues were guest-edited by poets writing from the subjectivities in question, something sadly less often done during my years in the biz. My decision to invite Philip Kevin Paul, Richard Van Camp, and Leanne Betasamosake Simpson to guest-edit the *Malahat*'s "Indigenous Perspectives" in 2016 was for me a watershed experience.

When I ceded editorial control to others, the world became bigger—something I wish I had realized at the beginning rather than near the end of my career as a literary magazine editor. Unlike many magazines whose editorial boards are often small and homogeneous, *Room*'s forty-member collective showcases a remarkable intersectionality. This team didn't need to put out a call for Indigenous reinforcements to edit "Indigenous Brilliances."

Meanwhile, since I left the *Malahat,* the number of Canadian online journals has increased substantially. With a few exceptions, like *The Puritan* and Sheridan College's *Ampersand Review,* whose inaugural issue I had the pleasure of reading, most online journals flourish outside the thrall of the official funding environment and therefore do not have to engage in the culture of appeasement that earning the support of granting agencies would have forced upon them. They exemplify what the internet is meant for: the creation of community that cuts across barriers like geography and even time. Unlike a print issue, which is withdrawn from circulation as soon as the next one appears, online issues are permanently accessible—that is, unless they're behind a paywall. These magazines are products of love, often run by one or two people smart enough to know it's best to keep them small by publishing no more than eight or ten writers in each issue. With the exception of magazines like *Train* and *periodicities,* which post new content voluminously if erratically, the hand-crafted, DIY footprint of most online magazines gives them a boutique feel, which adds further lustre to the joy of being published in them. Eight of the fifty poems I chose for *BCP* initially appeared in these magazines: Eva H.D.'s "Dear Ranchers, Wolves Are Kind" and Randy Lundy's "A Note on the Use of the Term *Genocide*" (from *The Ampersand Review*); Susan Gillis's "Oxblood" (*Juniper*); Elee Kraljii Gardiner's "A Mirror of Hieronymus Bosch" (*long con*); Jordan Mounteer's "Coyote (*Canis latrans*)" (*The Maynard*); Evelyna Ekoko-Kay's "tattoo ideas" (*The Puritan*); Nedda Sarshar's "Why did we bury the ashes?" (*The / temz / Review*); and Karl Jirgens's "Father's Day: *Homage to Robert Kroetsch*" (*Typescript*). I encourage everyone to support these wonderful online journals by reading, submitting to, and giving money to them. They grasp the big issues of the day with a lightness and a worldliness that Canada's burnout-inducing and sometimes soul-destroying funding models eventually make it harder to sustain. They remind me of why I became motivated to edit literary magazines in the first place: love.

Soon after I began reading through the magazines I was being sent like care packages to the front, I encountered "Angels 215> 1820–1979," the first poem I felt to be essential. Louise Bernice Halfe—Skydancer, by writing simply and achingly about the unmarked graves discovered using ground-penetrating radar around former residential schools, returns life and agency to the unnamed and the lost. Should her concluding lines—"Listen. Act. / These children are ours. / Could be…………………Yours."—strike you to be an excessive call on your sympathies because they've already been adequately stirred by the stanzas they follow and consequently need no further solicitation, you should ask yourself if you are to be trusted to do more than simply feel before turning the page. Another poet might have erred on the side of discretion, believing the beautiful lines that these ones follow speak loudly enough. Halfe claims no such privilege for her lines. It's only just now that many readers like me have truly begun to acknowledge the pain and anger behind what she's written on behalf of so many Indigenous peoples. It's understandable that Canada's current Parliamentary Poet ends this poem so emphatically—in this case, the rhetoric is more than validating; it gives voice to long-felt hurt and angry frustration. For additional information, turn to Randy Lundy's "A Note on the Use of the Term *Genocide*," which asks who has the authority to speak or, more importantly, the strength to speak—and if, as an Indigenous person (for this poem, unlike Halfe's, is primarily directed at Indigenous people), you do decide to give voice to your experience of genocide, Lundy asks you not to sublimate your motives in images drawn from "trees and birds / or dogs, or the violence of your childhood home," not in other words to write a poem of benign eloquence, but to speak directly, as Halfe has, and to remember "the pain we each carry, brother or sister, / the pain in every brown face, is not just our own."

Poems by Tawahum Bige, Samantha Nock, and Michelle Porter navigate similar terrains with different tonalities, while Susan Braley's "He Thinks It's Their First Book" and Laurie D. Graham's "Calling It Back to Me" pick up the other shoe of reconciliation by shouldering the kind of work that settlers must do in order to come to grips with the genocidal pain our ancestors have imposed upon First Peoples since our arrival on this continent over five hundred years ago, pain we continue adding to *in extremis* the longer we do nothing of substance in response—most significantly, the return of land (the writing of poems gives back psychic space only). However tentatively, both Graham and Braley go where many of us settlers still fear to tread—because we know our blundering steps shall understandably always be judged.

Moments of pushing back against validating rhetoric do on occasion surface in some of the poems I have chosen, although what their authors rebut is less connected to the settler presence on Turtle Island than to the more general stigmatizing way in which some readers (and writers) permanently tar anyone who's made the mistake of falling within (and afoul of) their wide-angled sights and sensitivities. In "Cancel Culture," Penn Kemp appropriates the tropes of letterpress printing to explore the zero-sum stakes in present-day correctness: "To cancel a person now / means to remove / respect. . . . Leaving mere / palimpsest left / to scratch literate / out of obliterate." Richard Sanger, in "Release," drafts a contract freeing the poet from being held responsible for triggering the reader, should readers, if they sign, "acknowledge that / as the free and independent interpreter / of these inky impressions (hereinafter "letters") / [they] bear full and complete responsibility / for all such calamities as they [the letters] may describe…" I found "Release" particularly relevant because, in my reading for *BCP*, I noticed literary magazines now insert trigger warnings about their content. (Because someone once interrupted a reading I gave by shouting that I should have come with a warning due to my poems' homoerotic subject material, trigger warnings are a trigger for me.) Tyler Engström meanwhile takes finding exception to another, more violent level in "A Red Brick" by having his narrator be so entirely out of touch with their own motives that they don't realize they've thrown one through a shop window until after the fact.

Anyone whose jaundiced views smear these poems as collectively being a blancmange eruption of white middle-class friability should immediately turn to Jeremy Loveday's "On Homecoming." Arguably the most optimistic poem to be encountered here, its protagonist is a ninety-year-old gardener planting her vegetable garden in full knowledge that she may not be around for the harvest, let alone to watch her seeds germinate. It's perhaps here that the flower attempting to bloom in Conyer Clayton's "Pistil Pumping" can locate its self-esteem, a flower that the narrator of Stephanie Bolster's "Alert" can gaze down to in relief after terrifying herself by briefly losing track of her child in a playground. Maybe it's here that Lise Gaston's narrator can also come to mourn the loss of her unborn child in "James." And I suspect that the father in Susan Gillis's "Oxblood" would happily flood the nonagenarian's garden to create a backyard skating rink, as my father did almost every winter when I was a child, so that his young daughter may cultivate life skills by learning how to balance on a pair of well-sharpened blades. Perhaps the narrator driving through Jordan Mounteer's "Coyote (*Canis latrans*)" would give the widest berth possible to Loveday's garden and everything gardens connote in Judeo-Christian tradition entirely and disappear into the less freighted reaches of the permafrost.

Moni Brar's "She Takes Me Deep" provides wonderful insight into the experience of non-European "arrivants" (a term coined to represent non-white immigrants and their descendants) who likewise endeavour to understand the experience of First Peoples. It's a study in comparative linguistics between Punjabi and the language of her Syilx friend (the Syilx's territory spans the BC–Washington border in the Okanagan): "into her people's land / this stranger turned neighbour turned friend / points out antelope brush and grey sage." By comparing the Nsyilxcən names for water, sun, moon, and birds with their cognates in her own language, Brar has found a way to more intimately understand Turtle Island, stripped of what colonization has imposed.

Other non-Indigenous poets of colour in this edition of *BCP* bring forward the experience of living in a culture that still often fails to notice, comprehend, or celebrate what makes them who they are or how they see the world they rightfully share. The narrator in Helen Cho's "i elitere lyric poetry" recounts being poor in Vietnam before and after the imposition of Communist rule in 1975, being a refugee in a camp in Indonesia, and the risks of accepting passage on a "pirate boat" in order to find sanctuary in Canada—and how accumulating traumas attenuate the links to family and home. Eloquently written in what many would characterize as broken English, this moving long poem is arranged on the page in columns of text that, to my untrained eye, mirror columns of ideograms created by a calligrapher's brush.

Cho's poem is joined by Helen Han Wei Luo's "Consider the Peony," which documents the challenges of growing up Chinese in Vancouver; by Nedda Sarshar's "Why did we bury the ashes?," an elegy for her deracinated, Iranian-born father; by Bertrand Bickersteth's "Soil," an evocation of how certain ground holds the memory of violence; by Mobólúwajídìde D. Joseph's sestina "River Boys," a celebration of growing up male and Black despite undercurrent and not-so-undercurrent white supremacy; by Leslie Joy Ahenda's "To the woman with him now:," a glosa marvellously free of the form's often tired lyric underpinnings; by Eric Wang's "Poem after Group Text Anticipating Next Millennium's Sushi Date," a hilarious disquisition on the ennui and etiquette of messaging (perhaps the most "contemporary" poem in this edition of *BCP*); by Evelyna Ekoko-Kay's "tattoo ideas," a miscellany of the many ways we choose to permanently mark ourselves, body and soul; by Sarah Yi-Mei Tsiang's "Choice," a frank meditation on the pros and cons of giving birth; by Christina Shah's terse, gritty thumbnail "interior bar, 1986"; and by Elee Kraljii Gardiner's "A Mirror of Hieronymus Bosch," a celebratory, girl-on-girl bacchanal fuelled by snow and adolescent hormones along Boston's Charles River.

Two equally courageous poems provide insight into the life experience of the neuro-diverse and the "disabled" (the term that the Canada Council uses in its guidelines), subjectivities until recently seldom represented believably in contemporary literature, however compellingly they were skunked by Robert Lowell's "my mind's not right" or relegated under the dome of Sylvia Plath's *Bell Jar*. Triny Finlay's "Adjusting the Psychotropics" captures the never-ending struggle to balance brain chemistry and the personal and social hazards faced while attempting to do so: "When we changed my meds, I leapt from the rock face. I swam myself young again, pink and smooth and milky. I swam myself fierce and fiercer, queerer and queerer. // The friends said, You're more fun when you drink." Kathryn Nogue's "Thigmomorphogenesis" (which refers to how plants respond to the physical touch of wind, rain, and passing animals) documents the ravages perpetrated on the ailing body by helping professions that seek to correct (read "normalize") it: "I became familiar / with the cage of a wheelchair. // Decades in it have slanted my spine, / gargoyled my neck." My god, Nogue's descriptions are so sharply defined, the words themselves seem to contort and recoil. It's the most justifiably angry poem in this year's selection.

Alongside these poems, you shall also encounter a healthy representation of LGBTQ2S+ voices. The executive director of a major arts organization recently reassured me that, in recognition of the challenges faced by queer and trans artists, cultural groups nationwide on purpose now publicly foreground their support, in part to thumb their collectively raised noses at the Canada Council after it failed to include LGBTQ2S+ communities among the marginalized artists it chose to prioritize as being worthy of support when it launched its previously mentioned "new," "streamlined," and "fairer" arts-funding "strategy" in 2017. The Council even had the temerity to say its good intentions were now in sync with the Employment Equity Act. Because no federal government has amended this act since it came into force in the mid-1980s, LGBTQ2S+ Canadians are not among the groups it's meant to integrate into federally regulated "work places." In 2021, in response to a suit filed by its Black federal employees, the government announced that it intends to review and update its anachronistic approach to employment equity, mentioning the potential addition of LGBTQ2S+ communities in particular. Should the feds ever manage to do so, I wonder how many decades the Canada Council, which required forty years to come into line with an increasingly more outmoded act, shall wait before shedding its emperor's new clothes to rethink with genuine *gravitas* its embrace of inclusion. Literary magazines meanwhile are doing the real work by publishing queer and trans writers in ever greater numbers. Maybe the excellence of this writing will substantiate the magazines' "contribution to Canadian literature," as the policy gurus frame it.

Intersectionality of course comes into play in the writing of the fifty poets gathered here; the BIPOC authors of several poems either already discussed or to be discussed later also happen to be queer or trans, having contributed poems that perhaps less obviously foreground their sexual orientation and/or the nature of their gender expression. Others, like Jake

Byrne's "Event Coordinator Moving into Project Management," read as being entirely comfortable in their skin. It may take an informed eye to recognize that the encounter Byrne describes takes place in a gay men's bathhouse ("Sometimes you know / By the crackle of static in the air / The vibrations in the puddles / On the sopping sauna floor. / In the shower after"). Byrne feels no need to make clear what's implicit to some and not to others. Instead, he goes for subtlety, employed with a confidence of expression that relies on shared experience well past fear and shame. Meanwhile, building up steam of its own, Sophie Crocker's "nobody cums rat poison anymore" overtly bristles with energy: "& how do you define clean? as waterboarding / a girl in the world's longest river / until she too becomes either amazon / or alligator?" Lucas Crawford's "Pet Names" coquettishly hews yet another line as an entree to serious themes: "I hear you call your cat a sweet girl and I want you / to call me a sweet girl." These three poems by themselves make me wonder if the adopting of a *tone* is simply another satisfying form of drag, and it's taken the emergence of queer and trans writing to make this obvious? Don't you think I should be able to apply for a Canada Council grant to travel to the promising end of that particular metaphor? As long as I get dental.

Putting that bit of wishful thinking aside, let's remember that the LGBTQ2S+ community, though still often shunned, is nonetheless very welcoming to all forms of sex-based marginalization, and it is in this spirit that I call attention to Sarah Hilton's singular "coitophobia" (which means fear of sexual intercourse). To address her condition, Hilton's narrator visits a therapist: "where I lay / on the bed it was hard / to say each time where this doctor's hands had gone / to uncharted waters below the belly" (please note that the slashes are the poet's; she eschews formal line breaks to further express the body's aversion to being touched). By all measures, this poem reads as the bravest among the many brave poems I've chosen.

Still other poems by and about people as they age point to another policy deficiency that literary magazines knowingly or unknowingly attempt to address. From the first funding application I filled out for *Arc* in 1989 to the last one I completed for *The Malahat Review* in 2017, the Canada Council has invariably asked magazines to demonstrate how they support "emerging writers," a term whose parameters it has never once defined. Rather than maturing, writers simply age out. This happens sometime after they become the "emerged," if not the "established." After repeated rejections, they suddenly realize that book and magazine editors have stopped being interested in their work—work the Canada Council had supported through and after long years of "emergence"—and find themselves hung out to dry, often just at the point when they are at the height of their powers. Isn't the Canada Council wasting its long-term investment in the emerged by not balancing its obsession with emerging writers with more nuanced policies that mitigate ageism?

I found myself reflecting upon this absurd situation while rereading Tom Wayman's "Father Pier Giorgio Di Cicco Enters into Heaven." Di Cicco "emerged" in the 1970s and 1980s as one of Canada's dashing younger poets, one whom the Council constantly put on the road—I recall attending his readings at the University of Victoria when I was a writing student—and who wrote compellingly about love and his Italo-Canadian roots before he forsook the secular world and writing in the 1990s to become an Augustinian monk. While cannibalizing the internet to flesh out what I remembered of Di Cicco, I stumbled upon an obituary written by Jacob Scheier for Toronto's *Now Magazine* in January 2020. Scheier, a Governor General's Award–winning poet, had befriended the deceased after he'd begun writing again. Although he didn't disrobe, Di Cicco became Toronto's first Poet Laureate in 2005, publishing a poem a week in the *Toronto Star* for the duration of his term. At his funeral, Scheier noticed "several poets from Giorgio's generation, but few from my own [were in attendance]. His later work (which Scheier explains he prefers) had not received the same kind of attention as his

earlier poems." It was this observation that particularly reson-
ated with me, because of course Wayman and Di Cicco are
contemporaries. Struck by Scheier's observation, I find it tell-
ing that it's Wayman and not a younger poet—one perhaps
younger than Scheier was at the time of Di Cicco's death—
who felt moved enough to give Di Cicco his "due"—to borrow
from Scheier—in a poem that, unlike most published in our
very unfunny times, is as humorous as it is affectionate.

Other poems that foreground ageing include Karl Jirgens's
"Father's Day: *Homage to Robert Kroetsch*," which showcases
the ravages of dementia, and Colin Morton's "Tinnitus":
"For years I believed what I heard / was the microbiome of
my inner ear— / cells living out their lives in there— / and
I wondered about this thing called me." K.R. Segriff cele-
brates ageing's posthumous benefits in "The Grannies in Dew
Dresses," which imagines and celebrates the liberation our
corpses experience while rotting in their graves: "There is lit-
tle worth pursuing, nothing / needs doing."

The grave is a fine and private place, as Andrew Marvell
suggested in the seventeenth century in "To His Coy Mistress."
While reading poem after poem in magazine after magazine,
I found myself wondering if it was time to put a finger to the
pulse of poetry and declare the private poem dead. Very few
poems written today seem capable of locking, let alone clos-
ing, the door on the world. In fact, I believe readers feel it's
the poet's responsibility to let the tea they've just brewed for
themselves go cold and instead walk out into a world ravaged
by colonialism, totalitarianism, and climate change, to name
just three of its many ills that call out to be documented.

Sometimes what we bring to a poet's work is not even their
fault. For instance, Billy-Ray Belcourt's "The Tragedian" should
probably qualify as a private poem, but we allow our read-
ing of it to be informed by his Indigeneity and his queerness.
Somehow both change how we respond to his evident joy at
being in love; the intersectionality they impose perhaps make
his love seem more hard-won and therefore more triumphal.

Isn't it tragic that readings of "The Tragedian" must resist our tendency to make the personal illustrate identity politics? Shouldn't reconciliation allow the poem more dignity by allowing the personal it exposes to remain what it is? Armand Garnet Ruffo's "Observed and Observing, That's Him" meanwhile straddles the worlds on either side of the above-mentioned door. His protagonist, a handyman at work on the roof of a house, has "a bird's eye view" of a couple "getting married COVID style" in "the backyard across the street." His eyes (and drill) impinge upon what, under other circumstances, should have been a private ceremony attended by invitation only.

Maybe only Sandy Shreve's "Late" today registers as a legitimately private poem through its descriptions of a towel and a robe hanging on the back of a door, both "overlooked / until one sleepless night / someone rises and flicks on the light." "Late" is also by far the shortest poem I have chosen, a quality that by itself speaks volumes and reminds me of a line from Phyllis Webb's *Naked Poems*: "the area of attack is diminished." After more than a millennium of continuous creation and despite all the privileges from which they are now determined to have sprung, have settler voices (for the lack of a better description) and the English-language poetry written by those of us who trace our origins solely back to Europe come to this?

Acknowledging my unsurprising white fragility, I say happily: "Probably not."

Poets do, however, like to step through the door, checking the thermometer screwed into the doorjamb to obtain even the most superficial measure of the world prior to going out into it. We like to write poems that give a platform to our reading of any given moment's alarming high or low temperature. We're all susceptible to coming down with Extinction Rebellion, Idle No More, Black Lives Matter, It Gets Better, All Children Matter, and #MeToo.

In 2020 and 2021, the pandemic afflicted many a poem, their authors having caught the bug. Fortunately, the creative variant of COVID-19, having no biotic basis, did not spread to the mainstream population, though the often seldom-read results could have been as deadly as other, more identifiable variants. As I read through the issues piling up behind my bedroom door, I found that poems about how the virus isolated us did not automatically lead to any memorable epiphanies; something else also had to be at play. I put my guard up by policing the blood–brain barriers of my taste, which is always in danger of being tainted by the pathos of the lonely, if not the down-and-out. Yet four pandemic poems, including Ruffo's "Observed and Observing, That's Him" mentioned above, somehow inveigled their way into my final fifty (is "somehow" pinpointable in the genome of a virus?).

Two in particular queered the pandemic—an example of the "something extra" a pandemic poem needs to inoculate itself against infectious sentimentality. River Halen's narrator in "The Enemy" negotiates the predicament of being nonbinary while cycling through a locked-down city to a repair shop where they hope to get their iron "fixed." In "The Last Thing I'll Remember," Michael Dunwoody limns a portrait of the speaker's elderly husband, who died of COVID-19 in hospital: "After all, he was just an old man who ... published / him/ him poems before it was the thing [meaning, unlike Cavafy, he did not mask his same-sex desire behind pronouns like *I* and *you*] / ... who stopped coming to the third floor / hospital window to wave to me in the parking lot." How chillingly reminiscent of many early HIV deaths Dunwoody's lines are. To quote Wilfred Owen, "The Poetry is in the pity."

And what could be more pitiable than the horrors the people of Ukraine are presently enduring (I am writing this on Day 79 of Vladimir Putin's "special military action"). Until the Russian invasion on February 24, 2022, the poems in this edition of *BCP* had read as current. Now, many of them read as if they were written on paper about to yellow inside a time capsule someone had better bury. The sudden change of context in which we approach them has exploded the illusion of safety I have enjoyed stupidly since the end of the Cold War. Of course, the issues these poems raise, like the lives never lived by the Indigenous children whom Louise Bernice Halfe—Skydancer has memorialized so forcefully, do not lose any of their urgency because missiles continue to fall on Odessa and Mariupol. However, Jan Zwicky's "Far from Rome," more than any other poem here, seems to speak to the politics of the present moment as easily as it no doubt did to the politics of the moment during which it was written.

Zwicky's narrator is on a ferry at dusk, physically gliding farther and farther away from the world, but not emotionally or spiritually: "Again // there was no warning: a shock of sadness / rose up through me, pain like insight / but unshaped, pure force." Almost in passing, the pandemic makes a nearly uncredited cameo appearance ("Far from Rome" is my fourth pandemic-adjacent poem): "the other few / foot passengers, masked, solitary, bent above / their tiny screens." The stars with the top billing in Zwicky's disaster movie are "the starving birds, the lice-lipped fish, bodies / emerging from the permafrost, jaguars, living, feet // burnt to the bone, the klieg lights on at Terra Haute, and the mob, the lie-stoked mob, / chanting its devotion, baying for revenge, all of it, all of us / roiled in that grief, sucked through the vacuum of its wake."

I can see the mob that Zwicky's narrator isn't able to leave on the cutting room floor drive out of the disquieting suburban nightmare that Patrick Grace describes so viscerally in "The Big Dark"; those drivers may have also adorned their pickups with Canadian flags in solidarity with the Freedom Convoy that lay siege to downtown Ottawa in January and February 2022. The fear that they're capable of stirring up would further agitate the man speaking his truth about the Holocaust while mowing his lawn in J.J. Steinfeld's "I Thrust My Left Arm Forward While Thinking of the Past."

Recall of one trauma helplessly triggers our collective memory of suffering deeper in the past. So many of the settlers who homesteaded unthinkingly on Indigenous land had fled the European famines that Rebekah Rempel recalls in "Potato"; and the Acadians rounded up and expelled from Prince Edward Island in the eighteenth century by the British in Adrian Southin's "*Dérangement:* Île Saint-Jean" would possibly recognize their own reflection in the mirror that Zwicky holds up to the twenty-first. The present (and the past and the future), she seems to be saying, is not something we can escape simply by taking the ferry out of Dodge. Despite all we do to skip town, "the world is too much with us," as Wordsworth opined in his own time. Whether we like it or not, that "too muchness" is what compels us to write.

By pure chance, since the poems in *Best Canadian Poetry* are alphabetized by title, the last one in my selection winds things up on a far happier note. In "You Are Story," Beth Goobie maintains that "the mind makes us in millisecond myths," even though forces in the universe may well aim to reverse this. By their very nature, these myths are lived "moments that transform you into metaphor's whim."

May all the poems I've chosen work upon you similarly, dear reader, and encourage you to think. May they also spur you to seek out more poems by the same authors while also turning you to the magazines from which they were chosen. To me, these poems are less the best of the year than ambassadors representing the groaning board of thought-provoking magazine verse published by Canadians in 2021. In *The Beauty of the Husband,* Anne Carson states that "beauty convinces." Beautiful or not, these poems convinced me.

It's my whim that you shall be convinced too.

John Barton
Victoria, BC
Lekwungen Territory

Adjusting the Psychotropics

Triny Finlay

When we changed my meds, I woke up. Woke up for the first
time in years.

The friends said, This doesn't seem like a good idea.
The moms said, Don't waste away on us.
The dads said, You're looking great these days. Can we get you
a drink?

When we changed my meds, I gave up booze, tried every
flavour of hot and iced tea, took friends for pedicures.

The friends said, Let's do this again.

When we changed my meds, I knew joy.
When we changed my meds, I knew grief.

When we changed my meds, I woke up and blew up and gave
up and threw up and stayed up all night, wondering if I could
be a teenager again. When we changed my meds, I leapt from
the rock face. I swam myself young again, pink and smooth and
milky. I swam myself fiercer and fiercer, queerer and queerer.

The friends said, You're more fun when you drink.

When we changed my meds, I woke up to the smell of
Guinness brown bread baking, Fundy mist on my lips. I
dipped, slept and wept, checked into the psych ward for more
medication adjustments. I grew tired of the meds, of waking
up and staying up and tearing up.

When we changed my meds, I re-read poems about love and
tea, about women who cry uncontrollably in bathroom stalls.

I filled books and books with the minutiae of psych ward life, some Prufrock and alienation: lists of snacks, plants, patients, setbacks, fish tanks, board games, peachy film on dank couches ... a catalogue of anxiety in objects.

The friends were silent.
The moms said, Let's try a new place for lunch.
The dads were dead.
The dads were always dead.

When we changed my meds, I ate wholesome meals and sweated to the oldies. When we changed my meds, I walked up the stairs like a curious fawn.

The friends were still silent.
The moms said, Come over for pie.
The dead dads drank craft beer.

When we changed my meds, I walked off a ledge backwards, certain, uncertain. When we changed my meds, I fell into a soft mallow field.

The friends were no longer friends.
The moms said, Can you hold the baby while I pour the coffee?
The family said, Never a dull moment.

When we changed my meds, I woke up, grew up, swam to the edge of a roiling infinity pool, the St. Lawrence wavering just beyond the snow's bliss. There was frost on the railing and steam at my eyes and I let the salt water heal me, not settling into the mineral abyss, not letting go.

— from *untethered*

Alert

Stephanie Bolster

When she was not there in the sand and not there
on the slide and not
there was a film in which everything ended.
A car drove out of the lot
and it was too late all
over while we'd talked, my friend's girls
nearby mine cupping sand
through her fingers until where?
Meanwhile no one who'd been watching
who'd noticed my eyes not on her
lunged to take her hand and lead her off.
She'd passed the splash pad the sand pit
the fish slide all the way to the red
tunnel she didn't understand my face
said *But I was here* and kept playing.

— from *The Antigonish Review*

Angels: 215 >, 1820–1979

Louise Bernice Halfe—Sky Dancer

"The Past Is Always Our Present"

A cradle board hangs from a tree
A beaded moss bag is folded in a small chest
A child's moccasin is tucked
Into a skunk Pipe bag
Children's shoes in a ghost dance.
A mother clutches these
Palms held against her face
A river runs between her fingers.

A small boy covered in soot
On all fours a naked toddler
Plays in the water, while her Kokom's skirt
Is wet to her calves.

"How tall are you now?" she asked.
"I'm bigger than the blueberry shrub,
Oh, as tall as an Aspen
Where my birth was buried.
See my belly-button?"

Each have dragged a rabbit to the tent, a tipi
Watched expert hands
Skin, butcher, make berry soup for dinner.
Boy falls a robin with a slingshot
He is shown how to skewer the breast
Roast the bird on hot coals.
He will not kill
Without purpose, again.

The tipi, tent, the log-shack are empty
Trees crane their heads through
The tipi flaps, the tent door
Through the cracks of the mud-shack.

A mother's long wail from 1890
Carried in the wind. A grandparent
Pokes embers, a sprinkle of tobacco,
Cedar, sweetgrass, fungus, sage
Swirls upward.

Children's creeks
Trickle in their sleep.
A blanket of deep earth
Covered fingers entwined
Arms around each other.

We have been
Waiting.

It is time to release
This storm
That consumes all this nation.
Awasis, this spirit-light, these angels
Dance in the flame.

The bones
Will share their stories.

Listen. Act.
These children are ours.
Could be ……………………….. Yours.

— from *Poetry Pause / Grain*

Attention Deficit

Tawahum Bige

Give me a breather. A spare lung. Some way out.
Need to quit smoking. Finish my degree. Mend
complex trauma wounds. Learn guitar. To cook.
A drum beats in the distance. I masturbate.
A drum beats in the distance. I come undone.
A drum beats in the distance. Edging is a gift
to get me out of bed. I've since taken a metal
detector to deep wounds. I've dug up treasure
troves, struck gold, kept going. Workshop
weekends. Smoked up. Waited to hear her voice.
Do I make it up? Contrive crush to soothe scars.
Do I make it up? Convince myself it will work out.
Do I make it up for a good story or bad
romance or do I gaslight my own ass
because I'm scared of rejection—only,
my spirit puffs his chest up and I am still here.
I rarely see my siblings anymore. I drank
whiskey, once. I've forgotten to water my plants,
kept them so far out of sunlight they began to wilt,
still alive. I grind my coffee for the French press
the night before. Except when I don't.
I've wasted hours taking selfies & editing shirtless
pictures I won't show anyone.
I confess a lot. God never gave me penance.
I confess a lot. I still drag my name thru the muck.
I confess a lot. And I didn't even do it.
The bad thing. The wrong note. The razor
over my wrist—I didn't even do it.
I wonder how much art I have made
out of my own Sistine Chapel. Out
of my own collapsing Notre Dame—it's on brand
for me to self-sabotage while others are contracted

to help me rebuild. How the art revels in the ashes
of a rejected Catholicism. I'm scared
of rejection. Of quitting smoking. I rarely
see my siblings anymore. Do I make it up?
Smoked up. God never gave me penance. The
wrong note. For a good story or bad romance.
A drum beats in the distance. Waited to hear
her voice. I confess a lot. Grind my coffee
for the French press the night before. Kept
them so far out of sunlight, editing
shirtless pics I won't show anyone.
I drank whiskey once, or do I gaslight
my own ass. Gift to get me out of bed.
Struck gold. Learn guitar. Some way out.
Out of my own Sistine Chapel. Out of my own
collapsing Notre Dame. I really want to show
this to her. How the art revels in the ashes.
It's on brand for me to self-sabotage.
I come undone. Some way out. A spare lung.
I still drag my name thru the muck.
Except when I don't.

— from *The Fiddlehead*

The Big Dark

Patrick Grace

Something big and dark has made its home
inside the wintered gas station out back. Did you
see? It entered city limits when you left
the funny pages for the dog to tear apart.

The school's been put on lockdown. At the creek
preteens build a three-tiered smoker's den
from vandalized debris. I've set alight
the hairspray from back then, small explosions,

rainbow-coloured flight. The big dark
has taken residence at Kingdom Hall.
The nonbelievers don't come back. Come back.
The town's gone

mad for baked beans and D-cell batteries
to power Geiger counters in its wake.
I wait in line with Bristol board and magic
markers. They say it's landed on the lake, its wings

propelling little hurricanes. How many times the word
"future" gets sucked under the checkout belt.
See what happens when they take our guns?
No animal lends muscle to intent.

When the town declares a state of emergency,
only the vulnerable remain. It's here, Magog.
I lift the interphone. The hunt begets the wait.
I've grown to miss the static and the fog.

— from *Prairie Fire*

Calling It Back to Me

Laurie D. Graham

Sinking through imagined
founding, across fault-lined

expanse. What wilts. What
mutates. The quality of soil.

Listing off a ship.
Two chests—

belongings
gone now,

but the chests remain.
Seeming crapshoot

of names until
you consider why

these are erased
and these retained,

why a name is carried
by many at once,

why we don't just have
our own to carry.

The hearth was cold,
and so, and so—

the stories nibbled
by our moment's

exacting microbes.

Touching a photograph
to discern what she

might have been thinking.
We mostly forget the names

of the towns that were left.
We don't forget the countries.

Borders heave; we
don't write. Sometimes

a family doesn't have
a story-keeper.

— from *The Malahat Review*

Cancel Culture

Penn Kemp

Between earning and learning lies
kerning, the name for the space
between letters of type to please
the eye in a proportional font both
natural and polished.

Not to be confused with *tracking*
where spacing adjusts uniformly over
a range of characters. And then
there is *leading*. And leading on.

*

To cancel a person now
means to remove
respect.

Check your Latin for
cross-hatching. Words
rendered illegible by
drawing lines through
blacked-out offending phrases.

Cancello, cross
out. Erasure rules.
Redacted. Where
do we draw
the line?

Leaving mere
palimpsest left
to scratch literate
out of obliterate.

    — from *EVENT*

Choice

Sarah Yi-Mei Tsiang

The ultrasound has pinned
your form—7 weeks: small smudge
in webbed light.

For the last 3 weeks I've carried
a leaflet called Medical Abortion 101
in the interior pocket of my coat.

You want the pregnancy?
and I say yes, if

       . . .

and I say: when are the tests?

     *

One time there were protestors
holding giant signs of bloodied fetuses,

all grey-haired and silent,
a closed wall.

The women were
already inside.

I hope someone
held their hands.

     *

The test, at 11 weeks,
will measure

the neck, floating stem
that curls inside me.

*

How could a mother choose to?
How could you?
could you?

*

My students discuss the ethics
of writing about others.

I write to you,
my other,

without knowing
if I will ever know
you.

*

It's a choice,
and this sounds so simple,

so I will just say that
the mother

in Pompeii
chose

to curl around
her child

and they are both
still ash.

*

My leaflet tells me
that after misoprostol

I could expect lemon
sized clots, fever,

cramping, nausea,
and that before 8 weeks

I wouldn't see a fetus.

*

The cross section
of the uterus looks

like a fancy cup,
something a Viking
would smash after drinking.

The cartoon woman
doesn't have a face,

and I'm glad for her.

*

I am a series of stacked
wine glasses—a single note
tremors:

an undulating wave.
When does the quiver
shatter?

*

Another 4 weeks
and you'll be the size
of a Lego astronaut—

lightly tethered
in dark space.

— from *The New Quarterly*

coitophobia

Sarah Hilton

every appointment was a prayer the healing came / quick
biweekly appointments in the Danforth from where I lay /
on the bed it was hard / to say each time where this doctor's
hands had gone / to uncharted waters below the belly he told
me loving was learning / how to float far from the shallows
pelvis pitched above the water- / line I learned to float the
way a marionette learns to submit to its / god I thought there
would be an ease to loving with the body / laid flat the lips
sliding open at the first consultation / doctor teaches me
the body is a lung / some places still need to breathe the
pelvis / hung midair the sting of strings spreading / the body
halved at the groin the falling / and rising of the chest at
his command / what is this body if the cunt can't keep /
me suspended she's got one hand on my stomach one / at the
pubic bone legs bare this doctor feels / around finds the
tension at the slit says it's about time / we give these muscles
a name / to let go of the hand that's got you strung up learn to
breathe back to grounding

— from *untethered*

Consider the Peony

Helen Han Wei Luo

It is for the lack of piety that
the peony pushes silken gold to the bees, their pilfering
seeds thyme and marjoram, and peonies no longer. This is
what lack of piety does—pollinate. The vinegar washes over
black wood ear, five spice, sesame, a full moon,
firecrackers, the red of my father's palm
lashing across my cheek. His hair has dwindled and
smoothened like a duck's egg rolling on the newspapered
floor of the apartment, cluttering against the jagged corners
for want of a mattress. Windchimes. My mother almost ran
away with a taxi driver, times are so bad. At the pawnshop
porcelain angels grin crookedly, all of East Hastings smells
of workmen and wandering cigarettes. I write because my
mother hits me if I do not, *I'll have a daughter if I must but
she won't be stupid,* she'll say. Now words are the agony
of a girlhood populated by star anise and fermented beans,
ground together roughly until the decadence of love and
brine simmered through the night. Hush, a boy is coming.
My father at the birthing bed, writes down characters—sun,
sea, riches, light, best of names for the best of children, an
enthused croaking lullaby, *When you grow up . . . I'll bequeath
to you all the volumes of our family history . . . You'll pass
them to your son after you.* There are no such volumes. No
wonder the peony does what the peony does. The enfant
prodigue has bathed in the whirlpool of wolfberries
and ginger. Marinated her skin. Now she drains the broth
through rusted pipes tumbling towards the sea, and seeks
no forgiveness. Steam rises from wild yam and congee, each
granule dangles in the liquid tassel of blinking lights of the
airplane carrying my family eastbound. I take a mouthful.
Wait for the bees.

— from *PRISM international*

Coyote *(Canis latrans)*

Jordan Mounteer

This stretch of road becomes a fact.
Like permafrost, so obvious it underscores

all other assumptions about topography.
Maybe it's the sigh of oncoming cars.

The Doppler effect of wanting company
that loudens as you near it and then

peters out. The drive-through coffee
at your elbow tastes like Styrofoam

and numbed cold hours ago, anyway.
Asphalt baiting you with all the tenacity

of a mother robin coaxing a predator
away from the nest. You survive

on skepticism. That what you'll find
wherever you arrive will be enough.

Telephone poles nag at your periphery
as a reliable measure of distance.

You come to things by increments.
Friends. Felt years. Degrees of both.

At a gas station in the slush beneath
the powerlines, footprints of coyotes

tow northward like electromagnets.
The revolving of the planet in their ears

a neural magic. What frightens you
is their obedience. That being guided

by the invisible is too much
like the leap of faith that love is.

— from *The Maynard*

Dear Ranchers, Wolves Are Kind

Eva H.D.

Wolves are good. Wolves love cream cheese.
A wolf walked my daughter home once, gratis,
without ever trying to steal a kiss or jugular.
Wolves laugh, too, just like coyotes and landlords.

Wolves are a great species. They have been captured
on film. A wolf can suck on hard candy without
ruining her teeth. Wolves are pack animals, they
have self-restraint, they need no toothbrushes.

Wolves have hackles just like the ones that stipple
the backs of the women that you, Dear Ranchers,
touch without asking; the hackles rise and rise, a wave
of encomium, awkward gawking of the tiptoe crowd.

Wolves love summer for how much it resembles
winter, its elder sister. They love homemade popsicles,
how the juice that trellises down their silvering jowls
is made of real juice. Wolves have a powerful thirst.

I myself have known wolves. Tone-deaf, immune to
criticism, abandoned and admired by the pack, in
equal measure, wolves I have known have failed,
repeatedly, to keep their word. The lacerations linger.

Wolves I have known to be among the best of wolves.
I have known wolves with whom I would trust my
ranch, wrench my right arm from its den of tendon.
Some of my best friends are men who dress in wolfskin.

Dear Ranchers, wolves are kind as their kind can be.
Their kits eat the same snacks afterschool as yours do.

They acquire a taste for blood as you did, hot wolf milk
scalding their infant throats. Like men they have been

known to howl all night long—and to die,
right on schedule, before their time.

— from *The Ampersand Review*

Dérangement: Île Saint-Jean

Adrian Southin

English soldiers marched with news that Louisbourg had fallen
and Acadia was no more. They led us

with bayonets hovering behind our shoulder blades
like a hull on the edge of collapsing; they were

practised at this, as were we. Sorted by family:
my Longuepées pressed into one ship, my neighbours

divided into eight others, three thousand of us
stacked in the holds, spun into hammocks

still woven with the odour of the soldiers, cargo for
the foreign shore they declared our home. This time,

there were no fires, no burning church like Cobequid, houses
left intact, barns cloying with fat, indifferent pigs,

fishing boats wedged in the red sand, rigging bound
and stowed deep in the hold for the winter, nets mended

for the spring, the emptied black earth stiff with frost, bowls still
on the table, everything in place

for the next set of hands.

— from *Prairie Fire*

The Enemy

River Halen

the enemy is you began to iron your shirt and the iron broke

the enemy is it's a pandemic and the stores are closed, the repair shops are closed

and more than anything the enemy is the fact you care about this at all right now, you joke with a friend—you like to make jokes at your own expense and your friends like that about you, how neurotic you are, caring about an iron in a pandemic and inviting them to laugh with you

so now the enemy is that friend laughing at you

and you think about the iron and its uses

the iron is for the shirt, the shirt to make your shoulders look square and your tits as flat as possible—you select your shirts very carefully for this, ironing them helps, creates an exoskeleton

so you will look like what people think of as "masculine" without always having to bind your tits, which is, in this pandemic as always, a risk factor for pneumonia

so the iron is for your safety, a weapon

the enemy your tits

the binder, pinching them

the idea a man needs a flat chest, that tits make you a woman, that these are the options so it's double edged—I mean, obviously

and broken—it can't fix this any more than you can fix it

you stood over the sink with a screwdriver and an oven mitt, trying things

and the enemy is that two months after the fact, when you finally call the repair centre (they have reopened) the person on the phone can either tell your iron is broken and your binder is in the wash or never credited those rituals in the first place, just the sound of your voice, "madame," they say, fixing you

yes, the enemy is that word "madame," the appliance repair technician misgendering you in a pandemic, increasing your risk factor for pneumonia

and you tell them your iron is broken

and he is otherwise friendly

and you can play this game too: gender that person "he" on the basis of voice, and their quickness to gender you, and the presumed fact that they are surrounded by working irons, wearing a flattened shirt, you can easily picture it

the enemy as imperceptible spray

so you cycle out to the appliance repair centre on a borrowed bike that is too small because your own has a flat (the enemy) and because public transit is full of the enemy too right now, in more ways than one

and so the enemy is the sun and the hills and your very own thirst, your legs getting way up into your ribs—you are wearing your binder, you are planning to show that guy, that person, just how flat you are, naturally

and you wonder how your immune system works at all, how it could ever stay clear on what to fight and when

and you know of course it sometimes loses track and gets it backward and people like you are more at risk of that, having an immune system that gets it backward

and the enemy is how much sense that makes, that the condition outside would enter, radiate through your relations microscopically

and a car honks at another car and you slip between them, invisible

lock to a post put on a mask pass through a door, sweating, put the enemy on the counter for the enemy, who considers it and you

and you tell them your name is not the one on the receipt or the credit card but a different word, and unlike most people (the enemy) they don't object or ask a question, just write it down—they seem gentle, if anything a little faggy

you would not mind to be seen as this person's gender, the way they look to your eye contains something of how you see yourself

and you tell them you find it tender there are places devoted to fixing broken irons still

you don't say "tender" you think it—you say it makes you glad, it's a relief not to be leaving your enemy to become someone else's problem, an ecosystem's problem

and they say places like this go out of business every year
and you will be without your iron for a long time because the
parts come from overseas and the borders are all but sealed—
please don't have false expectations, because many forces
oppose this work happening in any way efficiently

they do not say "madame" or you have learned to tune it out,
for this whole section of the poem you are blissfully untitled

you do not say "my enemy" or "biosphere"

and you think about the places like you struggling under a
particular kind of capitalism

a month ago your friend's roommate attempted

three weeks ago an acquaintance's roommate went through
with it

in six months someone close to you will hand you their
elegant folding knife when you ask, Is there anything you
don't want around right now

in the movies you grew up watching it was attacks from
outside—on a platform, in an empty lot, a person like you
turns and is strategically overwhelmed

just as, strategically, your work is circular and your tenderness
takes public transit to her front-line job

in another month, when you decide to touch again, she will
confess she wants to pay more attention to your tits than she
has been but something makes her hesitate, some symbolism
makes her hesitate

and you will tell her she is not the problem, she is exempt
from the problem, your tits too—this is a space for interactions
that are not the problem

and you say you understand, no problem, fold the ticket into
your wallet thinking about this interval in which to let/not
let the perfect, to sleep with, to be your own, to better know

— from *Arc Poetry Magazine*

Event Coordinator Moving into Project Management

Jake Byrne

His name was Marco. Sometimes you know
By the crackle of static in the air
The vibrations in the puddles
On the sopping sauna floor.
In the shower after:
An event coordinator "looking to move into
Project management"—*I don't know how to talk
To people with real jobs*—He spent his days
An ersatz priest officiating weddings
("Tall, Italian, bearded, I look the part,")
In this place that's all about appearances.
There is a love
For this blasted world that leaks
From my body hot and wet
In a tiled room choked
With eucalyptus steam, red light
And hyperpyretic piping
When every orifice of mine is full
With the warm promise of tomorrow

— from *This Magazine*

Far from Rome

Jan Zwicky

January 2021

On the ferry just at dusk,
        heading west into the winter sunset, colourless,
                the light behind the clouds, which stood above the hills,

great twists of clay, opaque, their edges flaring
        as a lamp came on and then another
                on the shore, I was alone

in staring out the windows, the other few
        foot passengers, masked, solitary, bent above
                their tiny screens. Again

there was no warning: a shock of sadness
        rose up through me, pain like insight
                but unshaped, pure force; it pulled

the stale air and the roar of engines
        after it, the starving birds, the lice-lipped fish, bodies
                emerging from the permafrost, jaguars, living, feet

burnt to the bone, the klieg lights on at Terra Haute, and the mob,
                                        the lie-stoked mob,
        chanting its devotion, baying for revenge, all of it, all of us
                roiled in that grief, sucked through the vacuum of its wake.

And later, in the small hours, at my bedroom window, woken
        by the faint boom of more fighter jets some thirty miles off
                heading up the coast, I do not recognize

the gauze that drifts across the black salal, the leafless alders. Once
it was called moonlight. Foreign, now, incomprehensible,
it fills the air and falls upon the earth.

— from *Brick*

Father Pier Giorgio Di Cicco Enters into Heaven

Tom Wayman

> *Christ came gently with a robe and crown . . .*
> *He saw King Jesus. They were face to face.*
> — Vachel Lindsay,
> "General William Booth Enters into Heaven"

I.M. P.G. Di C. 1949–2019

The Boss's Son, unfortunately—somebody in a white gown
holding up a clipboard
started to explain to Giorgio as, somewhat dazed,
he realized he stood in a vast, crowded rotunda
rather like, he thought, the main hall
of Toronto's Union Station—
no longer welcomes His ministers personally
to thank them for their service.
Too many scandals . . . well, you know.
But you'll receive an invitation,
if your paperwork clears, to a meet-and-greet
He holds for His recently arrived worthy servants
every few—
        "No problem," Giorgio interrupted,
still collecting himself: one moment entering
the rectory kitchen at St. Columbkille's,
and the next in a busy, echoing building.
"I never did get on with the hierarchy.
What I need right now
is an espresso. That would help settle me.
I presume the coffees here are even better
than at Arezzo or Florence. Only a couple of cafés
in Toronto make anything passable."

He grinned. "If the local espressos aren't heavenly,
I'll know I'm in trouble."
This is the City of God—the reply's tone of voice
combined shock and disapproval.
We don't have what you might call
'cafés.'
            "I thought this burg
was a reward for the faithful," Giorgio responded.
"Some reward if it's, what: choir practice all day?
Harp instruction 101? A lot of my poems,
which I'm sure you're aware St. Columbkille also wrote,
came from my favourite way to appreciate
humanity, that marvellous facet of Creation:
enjoying a coffee
all afternoon, talking to people who stop by
about their lives, their beliefs.
That's also how I began to understand
what a city is for. Who can love a city
that only makes demands on them,
that doesn't afford them what they love?
No cafés? I'd say your municipal government
is out of date. Every city should foster
a creative culture of encounter.
Not that cultural creativity can be imposed:
you clear away the obstacles
—legal, traditional, situational
—and the citizens' imaginations will work miracles.
Speaking of culture, does this place have
more than one official publishing house? Poetry
can only thrive if ..."

The functionary who had met Giorgio
was staring at him over the clipboard,
mouth ajar.

"Maybe I'm going too fast,"
Giorgio conceded. "I just showed up
so have a lot of questions. Let me take it
a step at a time: is there really nowhere around
I can find an espresso?"

— from *The New Quarterly*

Fathers Day
Homage to Robert Kroetsch

Karl Jirgens

1.

It's Father's Day again. In my dreams, I see my father, standing
there, surveying, theodolite atop a tripod. Up in Sudbury.
Now, he's in this place, in bed, aged 90, with Parkinson's. He
stutters, words break in his mouth, he can barely walk, when
he does, he staggers, falls into the wheelchair. He thinks he's
99. He's not. He thinks, he's going to work today. He's not. He
thinks he's late for work. He's not. His eyeglasses no longer
serve. He can't focus. He insists that his toothbrush must
be exactly 5.88 millimetres, no more, no less. He's lying in
bed, in diapers, trousers 'round his ankles, unable to stand.
He tells me he dreamt he walked around the room, walked
outside. Smelled pine-fresh air. He has no idea what year it is.
I tell him to read my calendar book, the date clearly posted.
He can't focus. He thinks it's 1989. It's not. He thinks he is 99
years old. He's 90. He thinks the clock is wrong. It's not. He
thinks he has to go to work. He doesn't. He thinks his wife
works every day. She doesn't. He thinks people are stealing
stuff from his bathroom. They're not. He thinks he's signed
numerous legal documents. He hasn't. He thinks I've written
my address on the wall. I haven't. I explain all of this to him.
He half-listens. It takes time. I think I'm going to get a parking
ticket. I don't.

2.

My step-mother insists on trimming his nails. She hands me
the scissors. He howls when I take his hand. I haven't done
anything yet. Be careful, she says, don't cut into his finger. I
say I've cut fingernails all my life. She says, maybe on yourself

but not on someone else. I don't argue. I don't mention my son whose nails I cut for years when he was little. I will trim my father's fingernails. Before I start, I get a paper towel from the bathroom to catch the cuttings. His thumbnail is brittle with age, doesn't cut well. She is pre-occupied looking at him. I have to ask her three times in increasingly louder voices if she's brought a nail file. She realizes that I'm speaking to her. Pulls one from her purse. I come to the index finger of his right hand. The nail is deformed. I remember the time he nicked the tip with a buzz saw, years ago, when we were repairing the garage. After I'm done, I fold up the clippings in the paper towel, flush them down the toilet. I remember the story my son told me from Skaldic tales. My son is now a teenager. He explained why it's important that people trim their nails. During Ragnorak, there will be an uprising against Asgard led by the trickster. Loki will visit all those who have died, in Muspelheim, the volcanic underworld, realm of the dead. He'll build a boat from fingernails he's gathered from the dead. He'll sail against the Aesir. That is why it's important to trim nails frequently, to delay Ragnorak. After I flush the nails, I re-enter the room to start filing, but I see that she's already holding his hand, filing his nails.

3.

I ask him if he wants a TV. He doesn't. On his wall, I hang a painting of a man riding a horse. He likes it. I ask him if he wants a phone. He doesn't. I think it might be good. He keeps bugging the nurses to call me, or to see if I've called him. He can't dial a number anymore. He can't see to focus. When I visit, I learn that he refused to take his meds. He told the nurse that if she let him touch her breasts, then, he'd take his meds. He thinks someone stole his wallet. He hasn't had a wallet since he arrived. It's been a year. He doesn't know what city he's in. He doesn't know what building he's in. He thinks we all live in the same house. He thinks my sister lives next door. He thinks he's 99. He's not. He thinks he's going to work. He's not. He thinks someone is going to take him to trial. They're not. He thinks he's escaped from prison. He hasn't. He was in his wheelchair, and somehow took the elevator down to the laundry room. He tells me how he escaped. He says he told the uniformed guards there that he was on the wrong floor. The uniformed guards were the laundry workers. They agreed that he was in the wrong place. He took the elevator back to his own floor. He says he fooled them good. He didn't. He thinks he's in Sudbury. He's not. He thinks he's 99. He's not. He thinks he escaped. He didn't. He thinks he knows the name of the building he's in. He doesn't. He thinks he knows what time it is. He doesn't. He's assured by the ID bracelet on his right wrist because it tells him who he is. I write the name of his building on a piece of paper. I write the name of the city on a piece of paper. I show him. He can't focus. I have to go back to work. He doesn't want me to leave. I tell him I'll be back tomorrow. He doesn't understand. I tell him his wife will visit tomorrow, too. I hold up 1 finger, and say I'll be back in 1 day. He doesn't understand. He thinks we all live in the same house. The nurses report that he had lunch. He thinks he hasn't eaten. He has. I smell coffee on his breath. I ask him if he had coffee. He says no.

4.

He is brushing his teeth when I arrive. I watch him for a long time in the mirror. He has the hot water running. He has used hair gel for toothpaste. He notices me watching him. He tells me they've got the hot and cold taps mixed up in this place. He says the toothpaste tastes funny in this place. He picks his teeth. He motions that we should talk. I ask him to come out of the bathroom first. I do not want to talk to his mirror image. He manages to sit in the wheelchair. Manages to get to the bed. Manages to sit on the bed-side. He thinks they keep changing the name-tag on his door. They don't. After lunches, he wheels over to the wrong room, to a room at the *other* end of his hall. He thinks they've changed the name-tag on his room. They haven't. I remind him of a picture outside his room. His is the only room in the entire hallway with a picture of a beach-ball. He forgets. Then, he remembers. He apologizes for being fresh with the medications nurse. He was. He thinks he's in the wrong room. He isn't. He doesn't know what city he's in. He thinks he's got to go to work, he thinks he's 99. He's relieved when I explain that he doesn't have to go to work. He gets confused when I tell him his age. He remembers when his younger brother was one year old. He remembers how they played with a wooden hobby horse pretending that one day, they'd ride a real horse. He remembers playing in the family garden with his little brother. He forgets that his brother died in the Gulag, years ago. Words break in his mouth. He says, he feels lost. He says he thinks his hallway is a dark tunnel. He says he doesn't know how to get out of this dark tunnel. I am lost for words.

— from *The Typescript*

The Grannies in Dew Dresses

K.R. Segriff

have paid their dues.

They sleep through the sunlight beneath
sheets of soil and in the gloaming
they rise, like bulbs, naked through the dirt,
and coat their delicate bodies in the moist breath
of the darkening day.

The husbands in bone suits
have settled for naps, they slumber
unceasing for they can't seem
to find a path out from their caskets
and the grannies in dew dresses
are not inclined
to reveal such secrets.

The grannies in dew dresses are through
with peace on earth, money's worth,
childbirth, hurt feelings,
carrot peelings and staring at ceilings
diminished
until the business is finished.

Their breasts do not distress them,
and have fallen like spent petals, dissolved into sod
—such fertile things—
and their wedding rings, lacking fingers,
now linger atop disappeared edges
of polished pine.

The grannies in dew dresses have let themselves go
have nothing to show
but bones without skin

for the sin that flesh brings
and names worth preserving
have all been consumed by the blooms
of a decade of diligent springs.

There is little worth pursuing, nothing
needs doing, and the grannies
in dew dresses shimmer in the peaceful pink
of the dwindling day.

They hold formless hands
and sometimes share kisses
because the bliss is
that little is forbidden or unseemly
in the spectral evenings
atop the fields greening
at Christ the Redeemer's Cathedral.

The grannies in dew dresses sway
in the loam, gossip and groan
about wayward neighbours
decked out in dresses of damp cotton
dropping despondent atop dearly departed
bone-suited darlings, clutching
their breastbones and fistfuls
of yellow gladiolas.

And if the moment is ripe, and fancy strikes,
the grannies in dew dresses press
their tresses to the failing ears
of their barely living siblings.

Don't despair Sister, they whisper.

Soon you get your dew.

— from *Riddle Fence*

i elitere lyric poetry   *Helen Cho*

— from *The Capilano Review*

that
night
in
sea
so
many
wind

but
small
boat

only   i   i
ten   always   cannot
metre   pray   handle
                                     because
we   please   just
are   so
forty-seven   let   small
people   me   boat
                    come
                    to   but
                    land   lucky

                    if   in
                    no   morning
                    land
                    i   we
                    .die   see
                                    land

                                    and
                                    that
                                    land
                                    is
                                    indonesia.

i always

i don't know why

my life

i always too late

i see people with no money
i try to help them

and then

i don't know why

i always have trouble sometimes

i always like that

now i don't need nothing i just live like that

when
i'm
young

i
know
how
to
upset
.myself

my
life

when
i'm
kid

i
never
live
with
my
father
and
mother

i
just
live
with
my
.sister

every
month
my
father
give
some
money
to
my
sister
to
take
care
me

my
sister

only
eleven
my
sister

but
she
take
care
.me

we
are
four
brother
and
sister.

```
   when                        i                  time
   i'm                         try                another
fourteen                       go
                               few                i
   i'm                         time               go
fourteen                                          waiting
   in                          one                for
  1975                         time               boat
   and                        some                few
communist                     people             day
  come                         liar               already
   to                          but
.vietnam                       that                    then
            that       that    time
            time       money    i                 i          he
                                still
            my         for     young             hear       have
         brother       when     so
           buy         we      communist          my         accident
          things       find     get
           and         right    me               brother    he
           sell        person   but
                                they             died.       died
           and         we       let
          when         can      me                                then
           he          give     go.
          make         that                                  i
          money        money                                 come
           my          for                                   back
          older        boat
          sister       so                                    i
           keep        i                                     don't
          that         can                                   want
          money        left                                  to
           for         my                                    go
          .him         country.                              more.
```

i
say

no   i
good   don't
to   have
.live   money   i
          to   don't
          buy   have
          soy   money   i
          .sauce   to   don't
                     buy   have
                     soy   money   i
                     sauce   to   don't
                     or   buy   have
                     .bread   soy   money
                                sauce
                                to   to
                                put
                                in   i
                                rice
                                to   don't
                                eat   have
                                with
                                .tofu   because

                                           it

                                           no

                                           .good

but   but
i'm   i'm
lucky lucky

when because

      i
left i
my   don't
country care

i   i'm
hurt lucky

i   because
hate
my   i
stepmother
because live
when
i   i
left
she   still
don't
give live.
me
one
cent
for
my
pocket
just
wear
one
cloth
and
.go

```
                              but                    i
                                                   left
                              i'm                    my
                              lucky              country
          when
            i                 one               october
         come                 friend                  4
         from                 give               .1982
          sea                 me
           to                 one                  when
      refugee                 address                 i
         camp                 for                  come
           in                 one                     to
    indonesia                 gentleman           canada

        first                 he                     it      i
        month        i        work                march      hear
            i       in        in                     30      for
           go     camp        manpower            .1986      first
    interview  already        in                             time
         with     over        windsor                        at
    australia    three                                       this
       canada     year        his                            time
                              wife
   everywhere        i        vietnamese                     my
            i                 chinese
        apply    still        so                             younger
                              i
          but  waiting        just                           sister
                              write
       nobody     what        letter                         died.
                country       to
         they       to        her.
        don't
       accept     take
         .me       me.
```

i
just
sent
money
home
for
first
time
and
my
older
sister
sent
letter   she
to   don't
say   have
                money

she
                so

killed
                she

herself
                kill

already
                herself.

                what?

                i'm sorry

                you want to eat?

                you want to say hello?

i'm sorry   my bird want something

                you want to say hello to my friend?

lot

of

pirate

lot   they

of   take

pirate   your   when   everybody
                 you   want
boat   boat   sit   to
                 in   go
in   your   boat   safety
                 in   but
.sea   money   sea   you   you
               you   have   cannot
         they   don't   no   choose
                know choice yourself
         take   where where
                you   you   because
         your   go   go.   sea
                                 and
    everything   wind
                              make   so
     and   you   you
                            go   go
     kill   where where
                            they they
    .you   go   go.

my				my	
stepbrother				stepsister	
my					
stepsister				sometimes	
sit					
in				something	
one					
boat	that	my		in	
	boat	stepsister			
that	bad			that	
boat	lucky	she	she		
eighteen		hear	say	boat	
men	wind	so	when		
four	make	many	she	she	but
women	that	yelling	wake	don't	
	boat		up	want	usually
usually	go	she		to	
they	to	see	she	tell	pirate
go	pirate	so	just	me	
forty		many	know		do
fifty	pirate	hand	she		
sixty	take	in	in		that
people	that	sea	land		
in	boat				if
one		she	she		
boat	put	try			they
but	eighteen	to	don't		
that	men	grab			don't
boat	in	every	remember		
only	sea	hand			they
twenty-two			more		
people	keep	but			kill
	four	pirate	only		
expensive	women	hit	four		women
that	in	her	women		
.boat	.boat	head.	.alive		.too

people

when

they

left

their

country   they

know

lot

of

people

die

but

you   you

need   don't

to   know

accept   where

it   you

go.

i'm fine !
how are you ?

good ?
summer coming

sorry

there you go

you want chicken ?
you want peperoni ?

you want extra cheese ?

okay   my friend

how is pizza   okay ?

thank you !

okay   one pizza   you want bag ?

okay eat here
you want drink ?

i need to put it little bit in oven   okay ?

hello   yes   sir

one pepperoni   yes   sir

tell me story   of   all these things

beginning   wherever you wish   tell even us

He Thinks It's Their First Book

Susan Braley

(The Cree Syllabary was authored by James Evans, missionary, in Rossville, Manitoba, 1841)

When he carves
his hands surprise him,
their greed for the oak:
hoar of bark, orbit
of heartwood, core of pith.

His palms are callused,
fingers thick
on the eggshell smoothness
of the blessed pages,
on the oxblood leather
of his Bible,
blood of the Lamb.

He spilled his own,
nicked his thumb
on the wood as he freed
its tongue. He believes
he will free their tongues,
his flock, with his book.

The Cree,
whose name means
the exact people,
will read.

Notwithstanding
the intransigence of the Company

who forbids the printing press
at his mission,
who thinks it best that Indian minds
be frozen like prairie lakes
in the vice of winter.
Notwithstanding
the snub of Bible Societies who deem
his "heathen" alphabet substandard.

Though bur oak is hard as granite,
the letters rise, bit by bit, beneath
his penknife, as native sounds
formed in his mouth months before,
at first imperfect, half-born.
These letters more than letters,
their simple shapes sing
this place: goose neck, owl's beak,
moose track, warbler's wing,
round of heel, curl of canoe.

On the next day, he creates paper:
the lining of birch trees, immaculate—
like the soul of an infant—gathered,
flattened and dried in a press
once used for hides. (He showed them too
how to build proper homes, abandon
those lodges of sticks and skins, thrown
together at random angles.)
His ink a concoction of fish oil and soot,
he blackens the faces of the signs,
the cells of the wood drink his elixir in.
At last he inscribes the characters
line by line, a syllabic system
a bright Cree would learn in a week.

Their minds break free,
like rivers in a sudden thaw;

they speak of him in whispers: the man
who makes birch bark talk.
They recite the commandments
in order, one to ten; they know
Our Father will forgive them
again and again. And the men
follow him in his tin canoe
through the roar of Metachanais
rapids to deliver the Truth—
        their grandchildren will stand silent in the laundry room
        at No. 17 residential school—
now they can sing,
the light in their eyes,
The year of jubilee is come
Return, ye ransomed sinners, home.

— from *The New Quarterly*

I Thrust My Left Arm Forward While Thinking of the Past

J.J. Steinfeld

Nothing like a sunshiny morning
and the annoyance of an overgrown lawn
to get me off my present-day despair.
To the task, fresh-aired disruption,
I cut the lawn flaunting its lushness
my headphones blocking out the whirr
klezmer music playing a little too loud—
Listen to this, Gestapo, I whisper
not from fear or a concession to unsteadiness
simply not wanting to confuse any keen-eared neighbours
who might not be pleased let alone understand.
Then I raise my voice so the Gestapo *will* hear
neighbours, mowing or lounging or lamenting untidiness,
will just have to take the baffling with the commonplace.
Back and forth, back and forth,
mower slashing the unevenness of history
contemplating what I learned
from unwritten books soaked in blood
from a mother who wouldn't step into an elevator
the memory of cattle-car confinement
concealing if not cancelling time and distance
from a father who would talk of history
as a vicious and harsh reproach
a ceaseless tabulation of endings.
During the mowing, morning exertion,
dialogue with witnesses and executioners
I thrust my left arm forward while thinking of the past—
Put the number on my forearm, I beg,
the number you would give her
give me now, scar my memory,
I don't quite comprehend chronology

wanting to share a bunk with God
promising not to fight over a ration
I need my hunger to see into the dark
when a young woman was in a bunk
no idea of a lawn that needed mowing
klezmer music through headphones
and a son's future conversations
over the morning cacophony.
Voices of the dead, articulate as the night,
I thrust my left hand forward again
deconstruct the words *Arbeit Macht Frei*
choke on the irony and my own freedom
demand to replace that young woman.
A neighbour smiles uneasily
not knowing I want to hide in her lovely house
just in case God has closed eyes again.

— from *Prairie Fire*

interior bar, 1986

Christina Shah

imagine boom, echo. your
underground father emerges
into a lean-to town
Ansel Adams' anticlines
bungalows and gasfoodlodging;
concrete cats crawling at their ankles

twin falls, one tavern. that men's den.
gold dust woman on dirty checkerboard
feathers, slipped fins flap
stiff on tanned hips
Eagles' epode warns sailors.

like you can move within a trap.

crew splices near misses with not a chance,
table populated with empties
butts with the wind knocked out of 'em.
he's dreaming she's Pegasus

she's mining time in grams

    — from *PRISM international*

James

Lise Gaston

This city's occasional snow demands we slow down
five minutes more out the door into its muffling
unexpected crush. I have been slowing since July
since the small pulsing furl of him stopped in me.

Name chosen in a sunlit instant stunned with weeping
in the hospital room, only one heart left beating.
A boy the doctor tells us, right before
numbing my belly, before the still unwritable scene.

We had been saving the surprise, assuming
a whole lifetime of gender.
Back in the birthing suite this bardo of his body stilled
but still inside mine, the choice comes quick as all other

unchosen in those cruel bright hours between losing him
and losing him: between diagnosis, black and white
and relentless, and the long push that brings him
into this world, to exit him into this world.

I first float *Cedar,* the room holding us, the only
reality I can render, also that heady warmth—
then *James,* your middle name but not on our optimistic list,
wary of vulgar variations. Now he will never have

a nickname we cannot control. Agreed in a moment then
a sound quickly foreign in the social worker's mouth,
she's trained to name what's already lost before
he enters here. The name of a chance

(everyone thought he'd be a girl) now written
on the certificate of remembrance,

the hospital bracelet never meant to fit, all the bits
of paper they give us because we cannot keep

what counts. You steal the tape measure that held
each inch. The sky's off-white as a page.
Medical instructions: take it easy,
no swimming: that last too late, came after

I had dipped my bleeding body
in the ocean to remember the sweet swell he made,
loss traced in salt. We thought he left
this world unmarked save the trace of ash, footprints

inked and smudged and rushing their way somewhere else.
Time rolls out like the tide. Small drawers
of his imagined future shut. Two months old today,
I would have shown him his first snow, the quiet light.

My reckless imagination. We didn't consider
how this name would be with us a lifetime longer
than his, just ended: the name my mother will
have tattooed on her calf, the name my sisters

will remember to say, the name on donation slips
in memory—The quick hot guilt that rises now
when I think how swift we were in naming,
how incapacitated. But when his soft and silent

body arrived into this unsafe world, feet curved—
unwalkable and perfect—he looked like his name.

— CBC Poetry Prize, 2021

kiskatinaw interlude

Samantha Nock

if you use the palms of your hands
to caress the muddy banks of the kiskatinaw
let your fingers slip through her silt
that is what i imagine it feels like to hold me.
this is what it feels like to be there and not at the same time.

the kiskatinaw looks like she runs slow,
eases around river bends,
has shallow warm pools
that will hold your body.
kiskatinaw means cutbank in my language,
it means get too close to the edge
and you will fall in.

i wonder what it feels like to be both a mighty and tender thing?

the river never has to apologize for the space she takes up
wide shores hold life.
deep water cuts away at rock.
pulls trees into her arms by their roots.
she is so gentle in parts
and so vicious in others.
enter at the wrong place and an undercurrent will bring you down
    into her depths.

she never apologizes.
takes you as an offering,
and continues to flow just as she did the day before and the day
    before that.
i have watched my body ebb and flow
fold in on itself, expand, and consume itself whole,
broken bones and my boiled blood;

i have sewn myself back together where my seams start to tear,
wondering how much tendon and hide it would take to make a
    new skin.

i wish there was a better way to say
that i am jealous of a river.
but it's hard not to fall in love
with the way she tears away at her banks,
and rises after the ice melts each spring.

i know it's in my best interest to be as soft as her water but i have
    never been gifted the ability to be carefree.

i wish my edges
were soft enough for you to fall in,

the river calls me friend but keeps me closer.

— from *Room*

The Last Thing I'll Remember

Michael Dunwoody

Is how his hospital gown lost the battle
with immodesty, surprised
by my own glance askance after 41 years.
He waved without looking, so white his hand
a limp flag while they wheeled him feet first
through self-locking doors marked DO NOT ENTER,
out of this space of tears and moans and fears
where nothing's left but to pace
off the room while the emergency doctor reads
the Apocalypse. She tells me
there'll be no visits, till my yes-but-what-if
unzips a half-smile behind her mask and adds,
"We'll take care of him," never hinting
at the rising temperature; the rasping cough;
the struggle for breath; the chest compressions;
the decision to intubate given his age.
After all, he was just an old man who never
lived in a closet or waved a flag; who dared
peers and students to think he wasn't man enough;
who bought a house beside a dentist who wouldn't
treat gays; who married me the day after it was legal
and loved the us of us until he couldn't; who published
him/him poems before it was the thing; whose in-
laws in their houses and churches and on their Facebook
pages refused him their weddings and births and
burials, would not speak his blessed name,
that old man who stopped coming to the third floor
hospital window to wave to me in the parking lot
even though I kept it up for days and days anyway,
after they wouldn't let me in the door until it was
too late no matter how I begged and begged.

— from *Arc Poetry Magazine*

Late

Sandy Shreve

Just this, the way your robe hangs from the door,
and how the deep green leaf in its floral
pattern (pink on black) is answered in the towel
dangling from a hook below the mirror—
just this, the way it's overlooked
until one sleepless night
someone rises and flicks on the light.

— from *Exile Quarterly*

A Mirror of Hieronymus Bosch

Elee Kraljii Gardiner

Some miles from Salem I ran shoeless through the snow, spilling.
Red wine pinked our trail along the Charles River
    where my uncle died.
The city was stopped, muffled and snow-blind,
adults long evaporated—the city never darkens in a snowstorm
but becomes absent. We filled all the spaces
with our suggestions, we were hilarious and unregulated.
Somewhere in snow I lost my red flats. I loved them.
We were a bright gang, and everything was hysterical.
I reached for a girl—she was late teens, I was early.
Six o'clock ringing from Old North Church. Cardinals
and crows trapped in white. My feet never felt the cold.
She piggy-backed me over the Fiedler bridge,
I must have been singing. Our cheeks appled up
in the elevator. My toes left feral marks on the carpet.
Oh how they burned when they came to life and how I danced,
hopping foot to foot! I would do anything to make it stop.
She threw me on the bed and began to chafe them
and I rolled my eyes back so far I could see pinned above my bed
the tshirt Billy Idol signed for me at Strawberries Records and Tapes.
I giggled through yelps and she warmed my feet
with her tongue. At midnight we made rye toast,
tomato soup, gulping mugs of water so we wouldn't
have headaches in the morning. Our lips burned
dark from kissing. When we woke up
the plows were doing their work, scraping.
Phones ringing, everything ordinary again.

    — from *long con magazine*

nobody cums rat poison anymore

Sophie Crocker

do they want us to starve. i did a bad thing;
i wore a bad thing's coat. to wash everything at once
requires nakedness. so you stand by the washing machine
& i kneel in front of the rinse cycle.
i am trying to perform unloving; a monologue, the opposite
    of a blow
job. i flinch at the name
birthmark.

& how do you define clean? as waterboarding
a girl in the world's longest river
until she too becomes either amazon
or alligator? does clean
mean all my ex-lovers are selkies
& i owe them their sweaters back? i throw patrick's housekeys
in a wishing well,   lose jason's mitten
in a cursed swamp,   sell ella's false eyelashes
to malevolent fairies as prosthetic wings.

i am more attainable than any other object
because i have desires. i am a slut, or i wear a slut's
nothingness. maybe if i turn enough other mouths inside out
you will become negative space.

rinsecycle rinsecycle, maybe i will move with water
in order to evaporate. liquid
i will have no hands for it. let me give nixies u.t.i.s. or instead
    of all this,
why don't we hide in the dryer
& suffocate like kids?

please hold me like a fleet of piranhas!

please love me like i'll return
infinity times! nobody cums barbed wire
anymore. it's like they want me intact!
if love doesn't kill me something worse than love will.
what's better? i wish i could want you less than you want me
but a wish is a want
is a havoc is a portuguese man-of-war.

come dawn
there's more left than i'd expect: lint, the smell of lemon,
one of your socks. still,
you don't cum acid rain anymore—
are you trying to knock me up? i am redunding the same ideas
with different intonations. sure, the shape of an umbrella
outlines the eightfold path to rainclouds. sure,
you leave every room like someone without fingerprints, like a
        chess player:
touch-move, touch-take. but if redemption is newness then where
is the newness in that?

— from *Contemporary Verse 2*

A Note on the Use of the Term *Genocide*

Randy Lundy

A few, scattered flakes of snow,
and you want to say they drift down
like ash from the chimneys of Auschwitz
or Birkenau, but you cannot claim that
history. Perhaps you have no right even
to write a poem in the long shadow of that
time.

And what of the sixty million dead in the Americas
in the first hundred years after contact? But that's
too abstract. Just statistics.

And you'll be accused of confusing, of conflating.
Let it be so.

                           What about the hands
of each and every woman who had her child ripped
away from her by disease, hunger, or by another's hands?
(It still goes on today.)

Can you write about that? What about those trembling
hands? A trembling like nothing you can say, not in this
or any other language, no words for that kind of pain.

Let's do the math: that's six hundred thousand dead each
year; fifty thousand dead per month; twelve thousand dead
per week, almost two thousand dead each day.

Four thousand hands trembling with loss every day.

Perhaps it is impossible to write a poem about such things.
Certainly, if you try, you should not speak of trees and birds

or dogs, or the violence of your childhood home. Your Irish-Norwegian father. Your nehiyaw mother. And fifty years later, you, still just a frightened, confused three-year-old boy. Do not speak of it. Do not try to make a link. Connect nothing.

Fortunately, most of those who might read this will not
    recognize it as a poem.
Still, if you managed to read this far, if you remember one
    thing when you reach
the end of this page, I ask that it be this: the pain we each
    carry, brother or sister,
the pain in every brown face, is not just our own.

And this is no confessional poem.

    — from *The Ampersand Review*

Observed and Observing, That's Him

Armand Garnet Ruffo

On a ladder balancing
off a roof. If you were
to look up you would see
a shamble of a man
holes in his workpants
holes in his jacket
holes in his sneakers. Holes.
To those below he is a man barely hanging on.
You can tell this by the glances
from the backyard across the street
where a couple is getting married COVID style.
From his vantage he has a bird's eye view
and he can see they are doing their best
to ignore the dark sky, to manage
their masks in the unforgiving wind.
A few minutes earlier the groom's mother
waltzed over in wedding attire fitted
for the cold weather and called up to him
to stop working. Rain coming, he said, looking up
and over, pressing the trigger of his drill
zoom zoom zoom.
But she was polite, and he acquiesced
tossing his belt of tools to the ground. Besides,
a thought had suddenly run through his brain
like a busy squirrel trying to gnaw into an attic.
Special occasions are rare at a time like this
and it was even more special
to be twenty-five feet in the air
looking down
on all that
hope.

— from *The Walrus*

On Homecoming

Jeremy Loveday

My 90-year-old neighbour is gardening again
She has returned to her body enough
To move her slippered feet from bed to the front yard
Where her hands touch soil like it was the first soil

Hands become water, a photograph, all the times
Her grandchildren visited, and it was joyful despite the noise.
I can confirm the volume button is broken on those kids
As it should be. Pack of rambunctious throats open with laughter

Tornado limbs breaking things with accidental velocity.
Over the fence, I hear rules to games
That are made up as the games go on.
Like all rules, I guess. But that is not today.

Today, my neighbour is planting daylilies
Which will work a whole year to ready
Each flower to open only for a single day.
The fullest expression of hope. The work of joy.

My neighbour, Sylvia, is tending to it.
Her walker cast aside, her pajama
Knees in dirt, fingers vining themselves into tendrils
Twining up her wrists, curling around her hospital bracelet

Toes bracing, becoming taproot, becoming anchor.
Fibrous shoots webbing out in search of nutrients,
She has placed a foxglove seed in her bellybutton,
Carefully she covers it with soil and mulch,

Sylvia is gardening again.
Even though her house is a rental

Even though she will never see the blossoms
Even though her grandchildren will not trample these flowers

And feel sorry, but keep playing as they should.
Even though, the garden will grow
And each year the foxgloves will reach the sun,
Flowers stacked taller, with Sylvia and her smiling

Daylily face making up the rules, whispering the game
Will continue, although it is not a game, that this year
She will be beautiful. She's going to bloom at night
While no one is looking.

— from *Funicular Magazine*

Oxblood

Susan Gillis

I've looked everywhere for the little movie of my father
skating on Frog Pond on a bright afternoon in 1962

grinning at the camera as he glides, arms spread, scarf
sailing out behind him. I can't find

the faint shunting sound as he chassés and turns
across sun-softened ice, as though he alone among

a whole neighbourhood out in the crisp air, sunlight
warming their faces too, gilding their hair too, knew

joy, twirling and cascading over the big pond
framed by the backdrop of spruce and pine,

shoreline rocks and dry reeds poking through.
My brother doesn't have it, my sisters don't remember it

and my mother let go of things like that long ago.
There's a moment before

the part where he's skating free
where he's leaning slightly forward,

holding two tiny mittened hands in his.
The camera loves his rough woollen khakis

tucked into socks, the dark red leather skates
cutting slow Cs and hourglasses

that steer him backwards while
the camera glides along.

— from *Juniper Poetry*

Parts of the Needle, Manitoba, Canada 1870

Michelle Porter

The eye carries the thread and the point penetrates the material,
either parting or cutting a hole in the fabric.

The sewing machine needle, hardened, chrome-plated steel.
Shank, shoulder, shaft, groove, scarf, eye, point.

The Red River, she threads generously across the land, offering
each narrow lot a fertile shoulder, a well-fed cheek, or a curve
of soil.

(For sewing by hand, the first needles were made
of bone or wood, parting the threads.)

The shank of the needle is clamped by the needle-holder, the
one God
or Gichi-manidoo. Where the shank tapers into the shoulder
are narrow

strips of embroidered land, up to three kilometres deep, with a
river frontage
of 150 to 250 metres, for water and travel. The needle either
parts the threads

or cuts a hole in the fabric—tanned deerskin, moose hide, or
cloth traded
from the Europeans, confederation. The shaft drives the eye
and thread

through the material, down to the bobbin. A bobbin is a
cylindrical spindle, like
the wheels of a wooden cart, but on which thread is wound.

On the back of the shaft is a cut called the groove, or provisional
    government.
The groove releases the thread into a loop so that the shuttle
    picks up the thread.

The scarf, also known as the Manitoba Act, provides room for
    the shuttle
to pass close by. There are different kinds of needles: universal,
    embroidery,

stretch, ballpoint, denim, wing, leather, metallic, quilting, serger,
    top stitching, twin,
Riel, Dumont. The eye of the needle carries the thread and the
    point penetrates

the material, either parting the threads or cutting a hole in the
    fabric.

— from *Room*

Pet Names

Lucas Crawford

I hear you call your cat a sweet girl and I want you
to call me a sweet girl. This is either the most or least
surprising thing. Tepid epithets are not our love language;
neither is the idea of a love language, or love,
or language—at least any notion that it works.

Sobriquet, another nickname for *nickname,* is French
in origin and means *a tap under the chin,* or, exactly
what you were giving your cat at the time, and ought to
give me, if you would be kind (of mine). Scruff my rough-
necked ways with blood-painted nails and I will lick your
ice cream bowl when I'm finished with you.

Honorifics seem horrific but at least ours neuter.
Nobody would have fixed us up, even though
we are both doctors who despise hospitals despite
the glut of hours we pass there. Men get hard to fix us up
with bandages, masks, and casts—things to *hold in*
when the quick of us is ecstasy. Escape.

I have made snakeskin of so many names.
Been multiple truncations. Of my last name, my first,
of THAT OLD PSEUDONYM. I have been animals of the forest,
of the sea, of all that is sweet in tooth and queer in claw.
I have visited your campsite at night when you forgot
to hang the food in the tree. People fear the dark
but predators bring on the day.

> Who will I be to you? Consider me on call
> for panicked mornings of the mind.

An ER doc once hooked teenaged me up to an EKG
just to prove that I was alive with thread-thin green lines.
(Should we file this under Cardiology or Art History?)
The machine had a factory defect, I presumed. Until
he showed me one odd skip in the beat. Then I knew
the machine was perfect and had read my end, worked a treat.

For the record, I am now
twice that age. Still I throb.
And so do you. And whatever
you call me, I will answer.

— from *Contemporary Verse 2*

Pistil Pumping

Conyer Clayton

You really ruin my self-esteem you know? With all of these *ideals*. I tried to have a supple petal, I worked at it, monitored my mineral intake, and I'm dying for symmetrical growths. But the sun always moves in the same direction and I don't have the luxury of relocating, unless you want to do it for me. But spare me that trauma, please. I'm not angling for root-rot here. I'm just saying I'll never be that daisy! That perfect yellow! A squirrel keeps chewing at my stem. Time requires us to drop leaves. Gravity spares no flower. Stop looking at me like that. I don't produce these patterns for your human gazes. It's for pollinators. Such never-ending expectations. Yeah, yeah, you're more likely to be chosen for reproduction if you're beautiful, it's fucked, this bullshit Darwinian world. What if I want to stay dull? Matte. Close to the ground. Laws of nature decrease my chances for procreation, well so be it, fuck genetics, I'll push my evolution towards androgyny and self-seeding. That'll show 'em. In a few million years, we'll all have our own pistil and stamen. I'll pollinate my own damn self. I'll present how I wish. But for now, pluck that pretty one. Anyone but me.

— from *This Magazine*

Poem after Group Text Anticipating Next Millennium's Sushi Date

Eric Wang

We throw a heart on it, because we adore food
& food emojis & food adoration. Thesis:
i'll feed you is the most romantic phrase
& all my friends are in romance with each other,
Typing... on the bottom of our screens,
each ellipsis a stop-motion of our hands
reaching, wound tight around goodness.
That's unagi, that's inari, that's Philly rolls
& discourse on cream cheese+sushi disharmony.
We're disharmonious, singing in mixed language:
all-caps, *just e-transfer mes,* faces cry-laughing.
We'll cry for anything beautiful.
We'll laugh for anything beautiful.
Cats, sushi cats, memes with cats building guillotines,
the text three days after M.K. met a boy at the protest:
just wanna [redacted] on his [redacted], so [redacted]
w/ a lil wasabi, i s2fg. Amen! o my inimitable prophets
of the blasphemous group text. Blasphemous
meaning no one loves us like us, if not but us.
Us, sharing our cry-laughter for food & sex,
our unaffordable want. Us, sharing Ubers
in our dreams to the places closed to us.
Us, here now, in the group text. Messy choir of sobs.
Typing ... : *i just wanna feed y'all.*
Us, with hearts to spare like breadcrumbs.

— from *Contemporary Verse 2*

Potato

Rebekah Rempel

Your roots, when they grow,
are thin and white
as an infant's bones.

You slouch in the cellar
in your tattered sack
like a beggar—

as if you are to blame
for all that hunger.
An entire famine

stoops to fit
inside your name.

— from *The Fiddlehead*

A Red Brick

Tyler Engström

I have a habit of collecting orphans. No, not what you're thinking. Just objects that seem lonely, you wouldn't believe me if I told you. I was walking down the street—my wife finds it grating the way I start a story—and I stumbled on a red brick. It was just sitting there, can you believe it? "Strange place for a brick," I said, but nobody was around to hear me. I picked up the brick and tossed it back and forth in my hands. It was a good brick, good weight to it, and that classic brick red. I thought maybe it had been in the movies, that's how good this brick was, but Hollywood was a long way from here. The brick and I walked down the street together and said hello to nobody at all. People started to look at me strangely, someone called out and asked what I was doing with the brick, if I was planning anything dangerous. I said, "I'm more worried about what the brick is doing with me, some things we can't control." I walked over to the corner store to buy a pack of smokes, American Spirits in the blue. I didn't really smoke anymore but today felt like all I had left. There was glass everywhere, which wasn't how this place was usually set up, and the cashier was nowhere to be seen. I helped myself to a pack and picked the brick up off the ground and brushed the glass off. I don't even remember putting it down to be honest, but it must have happened.

— from *Exile Quarterly*

Release

Richard Sanger

In taking up this wayward string of words
(hereinafter "Poem"), in a manner
either deliberate or accidental,
paid for or freely happened upon,
the Reader (hereinafter "you")
assumes all risk of personal trauma,
loss, or misfortune resulting from the lines,
images, or infelicities of said Poem,
including, but not limited to, acts of God,
real or imagined, high winds, avalanches,
lightning strikes, floods, the tree branch that may,
without warning, crash down on the café
where you sit reading this one afternoon
as well as all acts of human thoughtlessness
and cruelty, such as hurtful words or slurs,
black eyes, broken hearts, torn or soiled garments,
civil unrest, head-on collisions, war;
in addition, you as the Reader agree
to release the Poet (hereinafter "me")
from all liability, claim or cost
for any damage sustained in situations
that can be reasonably derived from the Poem,
extremes of temperature and emotion,
unforeseen desires acted upon, or left to fester,
any such altercations or contagions
as may occur or be transmitted
between consenting adults of any age or gender,
all resulting states of rapture or paranoia,
all losses of property or innocence,
all forms of disillusionment, religious or sexual;
furthermore you hereby acknowledge that
as the free and independent interpreter

of these inky impressions (hereinafter "letters")
you bear full and complete responsibility
for all such calamities as they may describe,
and are, for all legal and moral purposes,
therefore also the Poet (hereinafter "you")
and author of your own misfortunes,
such as they may be mirrored in the Poem.

— from *The New Quarterly*

River Boys

Mobólúwajídìde D. Joseph

We wake and wash ourselves in the river
our skins protest in raised dots the bite of the wind
—slashes of smiles, teeth bared in defiance,
us who struggle to swim, black boys
becoming men with booming voices,
backs to sainted trees haloed by a setting sun.

We bathe in the rays of a slumbering sun
baptized in songs babbled by this river.
Against the gathering dark, our visions take voices
that thread the dark cool twilight wind.
We who just wish to be brave boys,
bold and unafraid, sons of defiance.

We were warned away from defiance,
by worried mothers wary of the sun
in their sons, setting while still just boys
—doused in Marah, that bitter stale river.
They cast their branches cut by the wind
and pray for sweetness in melodious voices.

They will come first for our voices,
those who wish to break our people's defiance,
to turn us into tapes that always wind
back to before freedom. Who smudge our sun,
with smog, muddy with filth our sacred river,
who make martyrs of dreaming black boys.

You have heard of those sleeping boys,
the ones with memorable silenced voices,
hate of them—no—us all is like a river,
that rushes on and on in marked defiance

to loud claims otherwise. Like a constant sun
scorching the earth, suffocating the wind.

We wade in waters where trees speak for the wind,
boughs bending to cradle brash black boys
that float on backs browned by a warm sun
eyes crinkled shut by open smiles, laughing voices,
shoulders stretched wide with proud defiance,
bodies safe and at rest, made whole at their river.

Reap the whirlwind of our mourning voices,
we the boys whose blood echoes defiance,
us born of the river, sons of the sun-soaked Sahara.

— from *Literary Review of Canada*

She Takes Me Deep

Moni Brar

into her people's land
this stranger turned neighbour turned friend
points out antelope brush and grey sage
unwavering in summer heat
spear grass clings to our skin
as we wade through lamb's quarter
pulsing the want of seeds
through tufted vetch and shepherd's purse
capped with rounded clusters
while red-tailed hawks scratch the clouds above

into the valley marked by bloodlines
where dreams were swallowed whole
we skirt ponds that give life
to horned grebes, wigeons, and buffleheads
spot a lone merganser and a common loon
too early for blue heron to break
the glazed surface
we revel in the silent miracle of Water
      si'ulq, her mother would say
          pānī, my mother would say

up the notched hills
to watch wild horses roam free
careless and cared for from a distance
I learn palomino, bay, pinto, appaloosa
they twitch not for us, but for the Sun
      xai'ałax, her mother would pray
          sūraj, my mother would cry
and for the Moon
      sokemm, her mother would ebb
          chand, my mother would flow

onto forest floors I've not known
a cathedral of soft light
we count the birds
   naks, usil, kaƚis, her mother would sing
    ik, dō, theen, my mother would recite
walk beneath the watchful gaze
of red-winged blackbirds and evening grosbeak
there are no willows weeping nearby
just the sound of a black-capped chickadee
making its way home.

— from *Prairie Fire*

Soil

Bertrand Bickersteth

Now let's look at
a field
in fall:

half living,
half leaving,
half outward,
half injured

quartered
section
of parcelled
land

legally sub
divided
as playground

felled
to basic firmament.

Or

you just tell those
other
kids

no,

that
"black

is
beautiful"

warble
our parents
with worse-worn
worn-out
words.

But from here,
face to floor,
we see the molecular
sophistry of soil,

the *or*
of orthic
the *no*
of chernozem
the black
of *dark brown*

children

flat out,
face to ground.

Can we 'semble
this out?

A field is
just the fist side
of a fact

caught out
of season

and

found out in
words

and

in
jured

and

we swore we
would stop looking

at fields

because they remind
us so much
of absence
of beauty

it hurts.

— from *The Walrus*

tattoo ideas

Evelyna Ekoko-Kay

a heart weighed against a brick

a skull broken in the places that my jaw was broken

alessandra giliani cutting open a cadaver

a robot building its own legs

a cartoon heart with my own name in it

an octopus lighting a molotov cocktail

a stigmata growing roses

the community defence number

my parents' first apartment in back of the tailorshop

a pretty woman

an ugly woman

1312

the shadow of a skunk

a bottle of generic ketchup

pigeons hanging from a wire

the smokestacks of the hospital where I was born

a candle, lit

a candle, blown out

my lips before the surgery

my lover as a saint in triptych

assata's silhouette

a brain with the prefrontal cortex scribbled out

son house singing death letter blues to a jim crow crowd

a pig's head on a spike

the three bridges

the shipping routes

the ravine where the city workers got my ring back

a sleeping bear

an acorn with the moon inside it

a letter to my parents saying I forgive them

a match

a pair of scissors

a white pine tree

a bleeding maple leaf, upside down

the tower, falling

— from *The Puritan*

Thigmomorphogenesis

Kathryn Nogue

I learned to lurch, not walk, on legs
rigid as leadwood. Knotted muscles pulled me
up en pointe. Sometimes they twitched
electrically, pitched me into
furniture, walls.

The surgeons, blunt solutionists, broke
bones, stretched ligaments, sliced tendons. Sliced a few more
to see what would happen. My new legs
twisted outward at the knees, feet splayed like a duck's.
Even lurching was beyond me. I became familiar
with the cage of a wheelchair.

Decades in it have slanted my spine,
gargoyled my neck. One hip sits
two inches higher than the other and when I stand
I tilt dangerously.

A hundred years ago, I might've been displayed
with geeks and bearded ladies,
might've clutched a Fiji mermaid for comfort
when I slept in a carnival tent at night. Fifty, and I'd have been
boxed in an institution, safely unseen.

Today we're more advanced. Instead of pointing,
strangers stop me on the street to pray over me.
To ask how I fuck.

"A human spine," the physiotherapist says,
"shouldn't *do* that."

Look, I want to tell her, it's like this: bodies,
like branches, bend the way they're pushed.
In trees, it's called thigmomorphogenesis,
a slow response to pressure
repeated over time.

— from *Grain*

Tinnitus

Colin Morton

I read John Cage and, in a silent room,
listened to the low thrum of blood in my veins,
the hiss of nerves in my head.
Proprioception I called it, after Olson.

For years I believed what I heard
was the microbiome of my inner ear—
cells living out their lives in there—
and I wondered about this thing called me.

How much of *me* is a population
of microbes doing I don't know what
to or for me, living and dying
as I say these words.

Now I accent the first syllable,
call it tinnitus, as if that's an explanation.
I told the doctor, I guess there's little I can do.
You can complain, he said.

— from *PRISM international*

To the woman with him now:

Leslie Joy Ahenda

call us all liars
while you call yourself lucky.
Lord knows
I sang that song for years.
     — "His New Girlfriend Thinks I'm Crazy,"
        by Clementine von Radics

He knows what he has done.
Now you are hiding in your car & you pretend
the cracked windshield is making you tremble.
Maybe you forgot to tie your boots.
The snow isn't cold, or you're accustomed
to his disappointment. Your winter tires
compel you toward him in icecutting clarity.
There is only one way to survive:
get quiet, ignore me, obey him, deny her—
call us all liars,

I understand. I did the same.
You can only survive by wearing your skin
pretending it isn't patchwork.
Pretending it isn't mine & all of ours.
I know you taste his asbestos tongue
& I know your mouth is stuck. He
laughs. Peels back your ribcage.
Reaches through your organs
& grips your spine like a key
while you call yourself lucky.

For now, I ask this of you:
Survive. Drink water,

eat gummy vitamins,
hug your friends,
lie to him.
I know you know fear. I know
you forget you have hands
& you say yes every time he says
take off your clothes.
Lord knows

& I know
your yes is no agreement,
just how you get through
night after wretched night.
I know he pretends
he can't see your tears,
I know he mixes you a drink
& your defences dissolve
into a bitter lifeless cheers.
I sang that song for years.

— from *The Fiddlehead*

The Tragedian

Billy-Ray Belcourt

I am falling in love with a man.
It has been three years since the last one.
Summer after summer after long summer
I retreated to my commune of nostalgia,
my little lighthouse at the edge of the world.
Each time, I hung my heart up on the door like a raincoat.
Each time, I painted the walls a new shade of blue:
hungry sapphire, hungry cobalt, hungry lapis.
It was easy to pretend
the sounds of the brutal earth
weren't mounting to a foreign music around me.
Now, when he touches me
I feel like a poorly folded photograph
or a pile of imperfect orange rinds!
Oh, to toss myself away! To be an obedient blur!
To shiver in that empty, blue room again!
Why is it that love turns me into a tragedian?
Into someone without a history of solace or fearlessness?
Here's an hour inside which to age gracelessly,
the wall clock seems to demand.
I wish I knew how to be a person,
but when he puts his animal mouth to my chest
I think of slaughter.
I would be a beautiful wound to dance inside of—
what this means is that, there are mornings
in which I have to invent the concept of happiness.
It is ugly, ugly work,
and my hands are so calloused.

— from *The Walrus*

Why did we bury the ashes?

Nedda Sarshar

Because in the last year of his life, my grandfather dreamt
of mulberry trees and freshwater wells engrained in mountains.

Because in the garden, he planted
banafshehs and *nana* that my grandmother boiled for *chai.*

Because in the little apartment at Yonge and North York, there were
    only the sounds
of passing cars and the waft of leftovers thrown out in the lot.

Because no one else in the neighbourhood could make their tomatoes
    grow.
He said it was because they did not know to love their dirt.

Because he had suspected long before the diagnosis it was dementia,
his handwriting unrecognizable and head full of half-finished
    geometry.

Because he spent his youth in caves eating *noon* and sour cherry jam,
watching sunsets on mountain peaks his grandchildren would
    never see.

Because he had stopped speaking *Farsi,* and grew irate
when I could not respond to his slurred and country *Azeri.*

Because he taught me to play chess on the handmade marble board
in the garden while the sparrows sang overhead.

Because by the end he called me by mother's name,
stopped calling me *Naz Khanoom, Naz Khatoon* when I walked in.

Because I used to love to pick the cucumbers he sliced for *salade Shirazi,*
consumed with salmon and saffron sprinkled *berenge,* my fingers sticky and tinted red.

Because he told my grandmother they should never have come to Canada,
and that he wanted to die in Maragheh, on the same street his father was named after.

Because I once watched him follow a single vine until he uncovered the massive eggplant hidden between the thick trunk and fence.

Because he saved the eggplant and hung it from his wall, and I got it when we went to empty the apartment the day after after after

Because after we buried his ashes, I dreamt that we met in the garden and he
looked at my face and said that he wished he could remember me.

— from *The / temz / Review*

You Are Story

Beth Goobie

Principalities and dominions resonate under the bed,
press their netherworld claims on the mind.
The stairwell trails a carpet with a hunting scene;
the eighth step carries you away on the back of a stag
before the arrow strikes. Windows open like books
and a seagull drifts across the eye, lazy blue thought
with the universe in its wings; roses in the lace curtains
could be Jupiter or Mars. A feeling of coming undone
dust-speckles the air, tiny free-floating worlds
where yellow umbrellas enjoy the rain
and cleaning ladies trill in choirs of afternoon light.
On the front porch, your grandmother's rocker creaks
as she watches the neighbourhood stroll by,
an entire community crocheted, greeting by greeting,
into the afghan in her lap. The mind makes us in millisecond
    myths,
moments that transform you into metaphor's whim:
a peony's languid joy blooms you from the inside out,
petals unfurling and perfuming so you sigh and stretch,
smile at the blossom of your hand and think, *It's all a lie.*
No one kicked me out of the Garden. You are story
your internal organs imagine into being; while you sleep,
your bowels, kidneys and heart gather round a campfire
and confabulate new fictions, a caprice of plot twists
that rises out of the geometric design on your breakfast
    tabletop
altering the synaptic pulse of your brain so your plans for
    the day
shapeshift into a sailboat floating in a daydream of Mediter-
    ranean blue,

the toast in your hand a field of rippling grain harvested by
    peasants
intoning deep-chested folk songs about the legend of you.

— from *EVENT*

CONTRIBUTORS' COMMENTARY AND BIOGRAPHIES

Leslie Joy Ahenda lives in Toronto. She holds an MFA from the University of Guelph. Her poetry has appeared in *Contemporary Verse 2, The Fiddlehead, The Malahat Review,* and more. She is the author of *THRENODY FOR A DROWNED GIRL* (Moon Jelly House, 2021). Find her on Twitter @ljahenda and at ljahenda.com.

Ahenda writes, "'To the woman with him now:' is a glosa that takes its source material from 'His New Girlfriend Thinks I'm Crazy' by Clementine von Radics. The speaker of the original poem operates largely in subtext. She '[hopes] the truth / untruths itself,' hoping against reason for the new woman's safety. In the lines that I isolated from the poem, I saw an opportunity to address the woman directly and bring this unspoken truth to the fore. The constraints of the form gave me a framework in which to position my speaker, and that jumping-off point was exactly what I needed. I started by writing a couplet to end each stanza, and by finding an additional rhyming word for the sixth line of each stanza. Then, I wrote toward those words. It felt appropriate to use a poetic tradition that calls on others' works to discuss the topics of sexualized violence, intimate partner violence, and abuse because it's so many people's story. It made sense to me to write about this subject matter in a form that emphasizes connection."

Billy-Ray Belcourt is from the Driftpile Cree Nation in northwest Alberta in Treaty 8 territory. He lives in Vancouver, where he is an Assistant Professor in the School of Creative Writing at the University of British Columbia. His books are *This Wound Is a World, NDN Coping Mechanisms, A History of My Brief Body,* and the forthcoming *A Minor Chorus.*

Belcourt writes, "I wrote 'The Tragedian' in a bout of love-sickness. It was a way of confronting my psyche and giving expression to the contradictory feelings that love and longing produce in us: a desire to be understood but also to be hidden away. I see this poem as part of a queer tradition of the lyric in which the self is put under pressure and the conceptual proximity of desire and destruction are made apparent."

Bertrand Bickersteth lives on Treaty 7 lands in Mohkinstsis, more recently known as Calgary. *The Response of Weeds* is his debut collection of poetry and was a finalist or winner for numerous prizes, including the W.O. Mitchell City of Calgary Book Prize (finalist) and the Gerald Lampert Memorial Award (winner). He currently teaches at Olds College and writes about Black identity on the Prairies.

Of "Soil," Bickersteth writes, "This piece is part of my ongoing interest of Black history in rural places. Many of these poems attempt to dramatize the little-known experiences of Black pioneers on the Prairies at the start of the twentieth century. My aim is to bring these stories to life by braiding history, geography, popular culture, and my biography all together. This poem emerges from a previous one in which a Black farmer sings 'Berta, Berta,' a popular African-American works song, from his tractor: 'can you hear the difference, darling? Seed, soil, weed, oi-yull!' The poem, 'Soil,' forms a strand of his song. It tries to break down the dirtiness of racism by breaking down soil into its molecular components. As is often the case, the closer you look at something, the less its origins are apparent. In this case, I brought my childhood playground experiences into view because children are so much closer to dirt than adults, but they look to adults to solve their problems. As immigrants from a Black-majority country, my parents were completely unequipped to help me against something they had no experience with. So, when it came to racism, I was the Black pioneer of our family. I had to learn how to navigate the ugliness of this place that had seeded me with its ugliness; I had to learn to find the beauty of the land that had soiled me with its soil. I am still learning these two things: 'Soil' is one example of this."

Tawahum Bige is a Łutselk'e Dene, Plains Cree poet from unceded Musqueam, Squamish, and Tsleil-Waututh Territory (Vancouver). With a BA in Creative Writing from KPU, Tawahum has performed at countless festivals, with poems featured in numerous publications. His land protection work versus the Trans Mountain pipeline expansion had him face incarceration in 2020. Check out Tawahum's debut collection of poetry, *Cut to Fortress,* recently published by Nightwood Editions.

Bige writes, "'Attention Deficit' stems from a desire to explore ADHD thought streams through full, extended lines of poetry that make deep leaps within the same single stanza. It represents the stream-of-consciousness randomness that ADHD brings alongside anxious thinking. But in the last third, the return of thoughts not yet completed or concluded emerges in a way that adds to the disorganization yet brings conclusion to the narratives present. It was written just recently after Notre Dame partially burning down, and that was meant to be a greater metaphor for Catholicism being the root of disordered thinking very separate from my Dene, Cree culture that would find a way to accept the gifts present with a supposed 'attention deficit.'"

Stephanie Bolster grew up in Burnaby, BC, and has lived in Pointe-Claire, Québec, on the Mohawk (Kanien'kehá:ka) territory of Skaniatará:ti, since 2002. She has published four books of poetry, the most recent of which, *A Page from the Wonders of Life on Earth,* was a finalist for the Pat Lowther Award. Editor of *The Best Canadian Poetry in English 2008,* she teaches creative writing at Concordia University.

Of "Alert," Bolster writes, "After giving birth, most feel jubilation; I experienced an acute awareness of the fragility of my child's life and the certainty of its end. It seemed, holding her for the first time, that in a matter of moments I would be gone and her life, too, over. Hormones and blood loss? Or a rare glimpse into existence on a cosmic scale? A few years later, a black hole opened when I believed I'd become that parent from a news story, who turned away from their child for a moment and came back to a devastating new reality. Fortunately, I wasn't that parent, but just as culpable. Writing the poem years later still, I wanted to render through skewed syntax and jagged lineation the flashing speed of my rush through the suddenly huge park's various sectors, shouting my daughter's name, while in my head unspooled a flashback of some stranger leading her by the hand. Could anyone around me tell the world was ending? When I found her, another clash of realities: my melting relief against her blatant complacency. The title came after still more years, a placeholder I kept for the word's range of meaning: adjective, noun, and verb; from attentive to panicked. My daughter, now sixteen, doesn't remember this, and I haven't asked the friend who was there. By making a poem of this memory, I've forged a private devastation, yet it's one I imagine most parents have felt. By sharing this poem, I hope we can be alone together."

Susan Braley lives in Victoria, BC. Her poetry has appeared in *The Antigonish Review, Arc Poetry Magazine, Canadian Women's Studies, Contemporary Verse 2, Literary Review of Canada, The New Quarterly, Prairie Fire, Room,* and several anthologies.

She was a nominee for the 2022 National Magazine Award in Poetry. Her poetry was also shortlisted for *Arc*'s Poem of the Year Contest. Before moving to Victoria, she taught English literature and women's studies at Western University and Fanshawe College in London, Ontario.

Braley writes, "'He Thinks It's Their First Book' arose from my musings about the body of the book. How does the materiality of books—their paper, dimension, typography—contribute to the making of meaning? My research led me to the story of book-maker James Evans, a Methodist missionary who, in the 1840s, lived among the Cree in Rossville, Manitoba. He invented Cree syllabics, fifty Cree characters through which the language could be written and printed. When designing these characters, reportedly based in part on Pitman shorthand, he created shapes related to the area: owl's beak, moose track, warbler's wing. Evans's instructional books grew out of the land; he etched the characters into end-grain oak, made paper from birch bark, inscribed his text on the paper with fish oil and soot. The Cree were quickly taught to read and write. Evans achieved his goal: they learned to recite Bible verses and sing church hymns. His syllabic system was adapted by missionaries to the languages of all First Nations in the Northwest. Evans's production and reproduction of meaning in his syllabary had profound implications, some written on the bodies of Indigenous children who, not very many years later, attended residential schools. He never imagined the volumes of Cree stories, myths, and legends that his syllabary could have made, or the oral medium in which they continue to thrive. Some Cree peoples argue that it was a Cree man, Mistanâkôwêw (Calling Badger) from Stanley Mission, Saskatchewan, who, returning from the spirit world, brought this writing system to his people."

Born in rural India, **Moni Brar** now gratefully divides her time between the unceded territories of the Treaty 7 Region and the Syilx Okanagan Nation. Her writing has been nominated for the Pushcart Prize and Best of the Net, and she is the winner of the SAAG Arts Writing Prize, runner-up in *PRISM*'s Grouse Grind Prize, honourable mention in *Room*'s Poetry Prize, and a finalist in the Alberta Magazine Awards.

Of "She Takes Me Deep," Brar writes, "This poem came out of a day spent with my neighbour, Dora, who belongs to the Syilx people of the Okanagan Nation. Dora took me on a tour of the land of her ancestors, and it was an extraordinary day of sharing and learning. We spent hours winding through a maze of paths through sun-scorched hills dotted with wild horses, hidden lakes, glorious plants, and ponderosa trees. She shared stories of how her mother and grandparents grew up, how they survived the Sixties Scoop, and how they've prospered and struggled through the generations in the Okanagan. It was a true gift to learn from her. Dora's mother, Jane, is ninety-two years old and a highly respected Elder in the community. The day left me reflecting on my own mother, and how, like Dora's mother, she holds much knowledge about and connection to the land through traditional language. My family have been farmers as far back as I can trace, so I've always held deep respect for land, but this day spent with Dora heightened my appreciation for this land we now have the privilege of calling home. This poem is also part of a journey to renegotiate my relationship with the stolen lands that my family farms in Canada, and how we've shifted from being the colonized in India to essentially taking part in colonizing activities in Canada. I'm thankful for the generosity and patience of friends like Dora who help me understand what it means to live on this land."

Jake Byrne lives in Tkaronto, also known as Toronto. Their first two books of poetry are forthcoming with Wolsak and Wynn and Brick Books in 2023 and 2024 respectively. Find them at @jakebyrnewrites.

Of "Event Coordinator Moving into Project Manage-ment," Byrne writes, "This poem's inspiration is fairly straightforward: I spent an evening at a gay bathhouse in Tokyo called Kaikan 24, in Shinjuku's Ni-chōme neighbourhood, where I met Marco, and we showered together after getting up to what one gets up to in such spaces. He described to me his current career situation, which sounded ludicrous to me, but I imagine most people think it sounds ludicrous when I tell people I write poems for a living. This poem is in a series exploring gay bathhouses and sexuality in general, topics I avoided in my earlier work, mainly due to internalized homophobia. In this poem, and in others, I'm trying to explore the tension between the fact that this world is filled with immense grief and suffering, and yet we can experience camaraderie, intimacy, and human connection in transient relationships. And that ultimately, all relationships, and all experiences, are transient, but it's from those we build our lives."

Helen Cho is an artist based in Ontario. She holds an MFA from Goldsmiths' College, University of London (UK). Cho's multidisciplinary artistic practice contemplates the ever-shifting emotional landscapes of migration, language, memory, and representation. Select exhibitions include Audain Gallery at Simon Fraser University (Vancouver), Künstlerhaus Bethanien (Berlin), Kumho Museum of Art (Seoul), and Magnus Müller Gallery (Berlin).

Cho writes, "The idea for 'i elitere lyric poetry' came when I finished my video *So Many Wind* (2018), which shares the life and history of Vietnamese refugee Tai Lam, who now resides in Canada. I began imagining the possibility of his narration as a text installation in a physical space. 'i elitere lyric poetry' is a step toward that imagination. During a COVID-19 lockdown in the winter of 2020–21, I spent three months transcribing, extending, and positioning his narration on the printed pages. 'i elitere lyric poetry' preserves his fractured spoken language, follows Korean grammar by omitting articles and capitalization, and acknowledges the traditional Korean style of vertical writing, incorporating a spatial sensibility drawn from the idea of landscape. I borrowed the title and the final two lines from Theresa Hak Kyung Cha's magnum opus *Dictée*, which is organized into nine parts after the nine Greek muses. In actuality, there is no muse named Elitere; Cha invented her as a replacement for Euterpe, possibly 'to critique the privileged place of epic as high literature.'* In choosing the title 'i elitere lyric poetry,' I wish to insist on recognizing the lyricism of Lam's fractured language, the epic quality of his narrative, and his personal history and its articulation."

Conyer Clayton is a writer, musician, and editor living in Ottawa. She is the author of *We Shed Our Skin Like Dynamite* (Guernica Editions, 2020, Winner of the Ottawa Book Award), *But the sun, and the ships, and the fish, and the waves.* (A Feed Dog Book by Anvil Press, 2022), and many chapbooks. Her poetry, essays, and criticism appear in *Room Magazine, filling station, Canthius, Arc Poetry Magazine, CV2, All Lit Up, The Capilano Review,* and others. conyerclayton.com

Of "Pistil Pumping," Clayton writes, "This poem is part of a larger hybrid project tentatively titled *Tenement,* in which a human being is continually reincarnated into already occupied bodies. In this poem, the being finds themself in a flower. This project's intent is, partially, to question our human-centric views on sentience and value, but in this piece in particular, I am playing with extending notions of gender and patriarchal beauty standards beyond the human world. Sometimes I am exhausted by our obsession with beauty and the gender binary. So is this flower. I wrote this poem while sitting on my porch, looking at my garden, a few days after a neighbour had walked by and picked several of my tulips. Of course, they stole the 'prettiest' ones. I am thinking about how perceived 'beauty' defines our roles in the world? How does

---

* Shelley Sun Wong, "Unnaming the Same: Theresa Hak Kyung Cha's Dictée," *Feminist Measures: Soundings in Poetry and Theory,* ed. Lynn Keller and Christanne Miller (Ann Arbor: University of Michigan Press, 1994), 43–68.

'beauty' inform how others interact with us, with perceptions of ownership, gender, and sexuality?"

Lucas Crawford grew up in rural Nova Scotia and is now Canada Research Chair of Transgender Creativity and Mental Health at the Augustana Campus of the University of Alberta. Lucas is the author of four books of poetry, including *Muster Points* (forthcoming with University of Calgary Press).

Crawford writes, "The inspiration for 'Pet Names' is a fourteen-year-old deaf white cat named Celeste. In the earliest stages of my relationship, my girlfriend and I lived in different provinces. She sent me a video of herself petting Celeste and calling her 'a sweet girl.' Against what I might have expected for myself as a genderqueer transguy, I identified with it somehow! (I should also admit that the poem was written in the context of wanting to refer to my new girlfriend by all sorts of affectionate nicknames but being intimidated to do so because she is sort of a badass.) Being trans and queer—having legally changed names and having responded to a host of weird and mundane nicknames throughout life—I think often about how we come to identify with a certain word. What is it that makes a name or nickname feel like 'mine' at the visceral level? In this poem, adopting a name or nickname at the level of your body requires relationships; counterintuitively perhaps, I think the body's absorption of a name hinges just as much on a person hearing their (new) name as much as on saying it themselves. We often think of new queer or trans names as solemn and solo business. In this poem, I see an alternative where the weird adhesion of words to bodies is also about creativity, spontaneity, affection, and collaboration. And cats. At least one particular cat. Who, by the way, has more nicknames than anyone I've ever known."

Sophie Crocker (they/she) is an artist based on stolen Songhees, Esquimalt, and WSÁNEĆ land. They hold a BFA from the University of Victoria. Their previous publications include

The Fiddlehead, The Malahat Review, Room, PRISM international, and elsewhere. This year they are nominated for the Pushcart Prize and the Best New Poets 2022 anthology. Their debut poetry collection, *brat,* is forthcoming from Gordon Hill Press in fall 2022. Pre-order and find out more at sophiecrocker.com.

Of "nobody cums rat poison anymore," Crocker writes, "TW: abuse. I wrote this poem while on the crux of leaving an abusive relationship. I was considering how all the fragile, short-lived, and imperfect relationships I'd previously experienced were still better than the psychological torture I was undergoing with my abuser, despite how much he claimed to care about me. A week after writing this poem, I broke up with my abuser. In this piece, I used typically vulgar and violent language to evoke feelings of punk and pleasure. I wrote this piece during one of many Richard Siken phases, hence the self-effacing, transformation-based language such as 'i did a bad thing; / i wore a bad thing's coat.' My childhood understandings of the rules of the world—those of chess, Buddhism, and folklore—are the framework for this piece. I use these rules to try to make sense of the pleasure-pain of sexuality and adult relationships. This is also how my OCD makes sense of the world: whatever happens to me must be happening due to some complex metaphysical law greater than myself, a law that is perhaps only conquerable through obsessions and compulsions. Therefore, if I am abused, I must deserve it, at least on some cosmic/karmic scale. This was a difficult notion to break free of. 'nobody cums rat poison anymore' fixates on cleanliness, romantic sacrifice, and self-harm-by-proxy the same way that my own mental illness does and, in its last lines, critiques and tentatively, questioningly breaks free of these fixations."

Michael Dunwoody (1938–2021) taught high school for thirty years and was a sessional instructor of creative writing at the University of Windsor for ten years. His work appeared in magazines such as *EVENT, The Antigonish Review, Polychrome Ink, Plenitude, The Fiddlehead, Prairie Fire,* and *The MacGuffin,* among others. Full of humour, sincerity, love, and fun, Michael Dunwoody left this world better than he found it, as a husband, son, brother, uncle, friend, and poet.

Evelyna Ekoko-Kay is a queer, Black-mixed activist and poet from Hamilton, Ontario. She recently completed her MFA in poetry at the University of Guelph. Her writing has been featured in *Held Magazine, Midnight Sun Magazine, The Puritan,* Book*hug's *Write Across Canada: An Anthology of Emerging Writers, tenderness lit,* and *Voicemail Poems.*

Ekoko-Kay writes, "I wrote 'tattoo ideas' in a workshop led by Dionne Brand during the second year of my MFA. Over the years, I've been collecting tattoo ideas in the Notes app of my phone, which is also where most of my poems begin their lives. Surrounded by fragments of lines, the tattoo ideas themselves began to look like poems. I've always been told that because tattoos are permanent, they must be deeply meaningful, and although many of my tattoos have ultimately just been pretty images with no particular significance to me (a jellyfish on my thigh, a snake enmeshed with a chrysanthemum on my ribcage), my tattoo *ideas* have always been an attempt to find images that will convey something significant about who I am in the moment of their conception. In 'tattoo ideas,' I tried to imagine what images would add up to who I am. What I discovered in this process is that my sense of self is deeply tied to my familial history and my experiences as an activist. In writing this poem, I was also searching for a way to write about deeply personal issues, including interpersonal and systemic harms, without offering myself up for consumption. During workshop, one of my classmates suggested that I should state where each tattoo would be on my body. Another classmate wrote to me that I shouldn't take that advice. Looking back, I agree with the second classmate. I like the tattoos better where they are: nowhere and everywhere."

Tyler Engström lives in Calgary, Alberta. He is a past finalist for the Writers' Trust RBC Bronwen Wallace Award for Emerging Writers. His first collection, *Think of How Old We Could Get* (Frontenac House, 2021), was a finalist for the Stephan G. Stephansson Award for Poetry. He currently reads and edits for *X-R-A-Y Literary Magazine*.

Engström writes, "The inspiration behind 'A Red Brick' originated during the protests of 2020 when, as an example of the absurd current state of politics and political commentary, the question of whether cans of soup scattered on the ground were weapons (being better than bricks due to ease of throw) or simply food to feed a family became a focus in speeches and articles despite the significantly more important and attention-worthy issues and events happening at the time. 'A Red Brick' was written to address our addiction to loading even the most mundane, insignificant objects and happenings with an almost otherworldly, higher-power weight and significance depending on the context. A brick can be just another brick in the wall, a sign of decaying infrastructure when lying among others on the ground, or a sure sign of coming violence when held in the hand. But the brick is still just a brick, it has no say in the matter. There is a question of fate vs. free will, and whether, by deciding on the significance of the thing in context, we predetermine every eventuality available to it, and on a grander scale whether we do that with people. In writing 'A Red Brick,' I used a train of thought, meandering inner monologue style full of asides and missing information. The narrator is unreliable, ready to succumb to anything, but ultimately what happens, in the end, is the responsibility of the reader and what they think of a brick in the hand."

Triny Finlay is a queer writer, teacher, and mother who lives and works on the unsurrendered and unceded lands of Wolastoqiyik. She is the author of the critically acclaimed books *Myself a Paperclip* (Goose Lane, 2021), *Splitting Off* (Nightwood, 2004), and *Histories Haunt Us* (Nightwood, 2010), along with the chapbooks *Anxious Attachment Style* (Anstruther, 2022), *You don't want what I've got* (Junction, 2018) and *Phobic* (Gaspereau, 2006). She teaches English literature and creative writing at the University of New Brunswick.

Finlay writes, "'Adjusting the Psychotropics' opens my 2021 serial long poem *Myself a Paperclip,* a book that explores my experiences with debilitating mental illnesses and some of their treatments, including hospitalizations in psychiatric wards, psychotropic medications, Cognitive Behavioural Therapy, Dialectical Behavioural Therapy, and Electroconvulsive Therapy. I wrote this poem as a way of coming to terms with the wide range of medications I've tried, and changed, and tried again, along with the effects of those medications and the stigma surrounding their use. There is so much trial and error in the world of psychiatry and psychotherapy, and there are so many variables; I don't think it's uncommon to go through months or years of experimenting with prescription drugs in order to find a treatment plan that works. And then something changes in your life, or in your brain, or both, and you need to start again. I wanted to capture some of the complexities and frustrations involved in this process: the obsessive and depressive nature of the illnesses; the unpredictability of the medications; the absurdity of not knowing what the treatments are actually doing for us; the adaptability and plasticity of the brain; the tension of others' judgments during these struggles; the darkly comic nature of mental illness in general; the hunger for stability of some kind. Which is its own kind of paradox—how do I remain stable enough to function without losing the mutability I crave and desire so that I can live a full and meaningful life?"

Lise Gaston lives in Vancouver, on the unceded territories of the Musqueam, Squamish, and Tsleil-Waututh Nations. She is the author of *Cityscapes in Mating Season* (Signature Editions, 2017) and the winner of the Harold Taylor Prize from the Academy of American Poets and of the 2021 CBC Poetry Prize. Recent work has appeared in *Arc Poetry Magazine, The Dalhousie Review, The Fiddlehead, The Malahat Review,* and *Prairie Fire.* lisegaston.com

Gaston writes, "I wrote 'James' for and about my son, who arrived stillborn in July 2020. When I was able to start writing again, six months after, it was difficult to put such an overwhelming experience into words. For this poem, I managed to find a point of focus through the aspect of naming. How do we choose a name when all the imagined, excitedly discussed names were attached to the expectation of a living child? How do we choose a name when the first person we will tell is the social worker who is giving us a list of funeral homes? We named him quickly, in the midst of grief and shock, in the short hours between his death and his birth. This poem is about that moment, but also what I couldn't realize until after: that naming has a surprising permanence to it, even while his existence felt so impermanent. It was a choice that has gone beyond the day of his birth and death, when we couldn't even imagine how our own lives would continue outside of that hospital room. I didn't know the extent to which my husband and I would carry that name with us. This is the most personal and in many ways the most difficult poem I have ever written, but I am grateful to have connected, through poetry, with other loss parents, and to be able to honour my son in this way. He will always be our firstborn."

Susan Gillis lives in rural Ontario. She has published four books of poetry, most recently *Yellow Crane* (Brick, 2018), and is a member of the collaborative group Yoko's Dogs.

Of "Oxblood," Gillis writes, "This poem began in several places at once, soon after moving my father into long-term care near the end of his life: morning light landing on a pair of dark-red leather boxing gloves on my bookshelf; the name of that colour, so specific and gory; the sudden recognition of that very red as the colour of my young father's skates; and a frantic wish to be able to hold in my hands something that was slipping away in the upheaval of his move. I've often had the uncanny sense that some deep memories exist as photographs or movies; this poem tracks one of those."

Beth Goobie has celebrated the last quarter century in Saskatoon, within the territory of Treaty 6. Her latest poetry collection, *Lookin' for Joy,* was released by Exile Editions in 2022. It was gratefully written on an SK Arts grant. Beth won the 2021 Carter V. Cooper Award for short fiction, in the "Established" category.

Goobie writes, "'You Are Story' started with an image of a carpet on a staircase that contains a hunting scene—as the protagonist climbs the stairs, they step into an alternate universe. A series of alternate universes, or stories, open out of this original reality-shift as the poem progresses. This is very like the experience of writing your way through a year on an SK Arts grant (which funded the writing of the poetry collection, *Lookin' for Joy,* in which this poem appears). Every day, I sat down to write, and a poem rose out of me and onto the page, a vivid alternate universe that created itself in my nebulous innards, then invited itself into my 'rational mind.' Every creator knows the inner kaleidoscope that is constantly in motion, shifting between possible patterns, and then the moment when it halts in a comprehensible thought form that lifts into what we call consciousness. After a year of this, you do, indeed, feel as if you are story/poem constantly in the process of self-creation. Thank you to all provincial and federal arts-funding organizations that provide creative writing grants and the time for this oasis of self-exploration!"

Patrick Grace is a writer from Vancouver, where he works as an elementary school teacher and moonlights as managing editor of *Plenitude Magazine*. Recent poems have appeared in *The Fiddlehead, EVENT, The Malahat Review,* and *The Puritan.* His first chapbook, *Dastardly,* was published with Anstruther Press in late 2021. "The Big Dark" was a finalist for *CV2*'s annual poetry contest in 2016.

Of "The Big Dark," Grace writes, "I wrote this poem as a meditation on grief after a sudden breakup. I had taken a little job housesitting near the ocean, away from most reminders of my ex, but I knew I had to write about him while the rawness was still alive inside me. My biggest challenge was creating a narrative that avoided overwrought emotion while emphasizing that initial shock we feel when we get dumped. The 'big dark' in the poem is a physical manifestation of pain that arrives in a small town, a literal monster that drives the townsfolk into a state of panic. My interest in apocalyptic stories was a source of inspiration here. Much of the poem is propelled forward in iambic beats, lending power in a push-pull of varied staccato and sudden stops to mimic my experience. My poetry often tethers the absurd as a coping mechanism, and this piece is no exception: the 'funny pages,' the 'hairspray,' the 'Bristol board and magic markers'—it's all so strange, but this strangeness was the only way to pull through and survive before the monster, the grief I had to face alone, finally came calling."

Laurie D. Graham grew up in Treaty 6 territory, outside Edmonton, and she currently lives in Nogojiwanong, a.k.a. Peterborough, Ontario, in the territory of the Mississauga Anishinaabeg, where she is a writer, an editor, and the publisher of *Brick* magazine. Her latest book, *Fast Commute,* was published by McClelland & Stewart in spring 2022.

Graham writes, "These days, 'Calling It Back to Me' is acting as an anchor for a series of poems that zero in on my great-grandparents—all of whom immigrated to the Prairies to farm in the first years of the twentieth century—and particularly my great-grandmothers: the circumstances of their lives both before and after they left their homes and settled on this continent, what's possible to know, what's gone forever, how colonization exists in and founds my family's stories, how it interrupts, covers over, supplants. This poem circles that break from the home continent, that gap, what caused it, its damages. The poem's short lines seem to echo a lack, a reticence, a legacy of silence."

Eva H.D. resides on unceded territory. She works in your favourite bar.

Of 'Dear Ranchers, Wolves are Kind,' H.D. writes, "This is a wolf-based poem addressed to ranchers. Which are you?"

River Halen is an award-winning writer of Catalan and Danish descent living in Tio'tia:ke (Montreal). Their poems and essays dealing with relation, ecology, transformation, and sexuality have been published widely in North America and Australia, and in translation in Japan. Their book *Dream Rooms* will be published by Book*hug Press in fall 2022.

Halen writes, "'The Enemy' is about what happens in a culture where people think they can perceive other people's gender with their senses."

Louise Bernice Halfe—Sky Dancer was raised on Saddle Lake Reserve and attended Blue Quills Residential School. Louise is married, has two adult children and three grandsons. She graduated with a Bachelor of Social Work from the University of Regina. She also completed two years of Addictions Counsellor Training at St. Albert's Nechi Institute, where she also facilitated the program. She served as Saskatchewan's Poet Laureate for two years and has travelled extensively for her poetics and to present at numerous conferences. Her books include *Bear Bones and Feathers, Blue Marrow, The Crooked Good, Burning in This Midnight Dream, Sohkeyihta* (a compilation of her work from Wilfrid Laurier Press), and *awasis-kinky and dishevelled.* She has received numerous accolades and awards including honorary doctorates from Wilfrid Laurier University, the

University of Saskatchewan, and Mount Royal University. She currently serves as the national Parliamentary Library Poet Laureate. Louise also serves as an Elder or knowledge keeper at the University of Saskatchewan and the Saskatchewan Health Authority, Virtual Hospice, Opik, and others. She actively participates in cultural and ceremonial activities relevant to her Plains Cree culture.

Halfe writes, "'Angels,' which is published on the Parliamentary Poet website in Cree, English, and French, was written after an Elder asked me to take into consideration the boys who were forced to dig the graves of their fellow residential school attendees. These boys have gone unacknowledged and she felt it was important for the public to know their trauma they have carried in life as a result."

Sarah Hilton is a queer poet from Scarborough. She is the author of two chapbooks: *homecoming* (Model Press, 2021) and *Saltwater Lacuna* (Anstruther Press, 2022). She is the recipient of the E. Nelson Poetry Award and was shortlisted for the Laura K. Alleyne Difficult Fruit Poetry Prize in 2019. She is a soon-to-be librarian completing the Master of Information program at the University of Toronto.

Of "coitophobia," Hilton writes, "From October 2018 to March 2019, I experienced my last heterosexual relationship before finally exploring relationships with women. Up until this point, I had never experienced fulfilling relationships with men, and in this particular relationship, I was dealt mental and sexual manipulation unlike anything I had ever known. I was made to feel like my body was broken as I was unable to perform penetrative sex with my partner without experiencing extreme vaginal pain. A month after the relationship ended, I sought out professional help and was diagnosed with vaginismus, a condition which can stem from repressed homosexuality. Almost immediately, I began attending physical therapy with a doctor who specialized in pelvic health. Though the treatment was helpful with time, I felt haunted at each appointment by the feeling of flight that entered my body as I was reminded of the instances where I was sexually engaged with my former partner who would shame me for my pain. 'coitophobia' reflects the emotional distress that racked my mind and body as I lay in physical therapy appointments and expresses my desperation to fit my body into the mould of a heterosexual relationship."

Karl Jirgens, professor emeritus, former English Department head and former chair of the Creative Writing Program (University of Windsor), author of two books of fiction and two scholarly books (Coach House, Mercury, and ECW Presses), edited two books (on painter Jack Bush and poet Christopher Dewdney) plus an issue of *Open Letter* magazine with Beatriz Hausner. His scholarly and creative works are published globally. Jirgens edited/published *Rampike,* an international journal of art, writing, and theory (1979–2016), now digitally archived (free) c/o the University of Windsor: scholar.uwindsor.ca/rampike/about.html. His short-fiction collection, *The Razor's Edge,* was recently released (2022) from The Porcupine's Quill.

Jirgens writes, "'Father's Day: *Homage to Robert Kroetsch*' was written in response to a call from *The Typescript* for expressions in honour of Robert Kroetsch. This text combines concept with technique by montaging film clip–like images of my father in his early nineties while confined to a nursing home due to Parkinson's disease. This prose-poem uses precise and repetitive syntax to suggest nursing home regimens, plus a disrupted mind-state in contrast with youthful hope and energy. The textual discord indicates a psychic discord, rife with neurosis, partial amnesia, and the erosion of physical prowess resulting from old age. The recollection of the Gulag blends the untimely death of my uncle with my father's eventual passing. Because it recalls colonialism in Europe, the Gulag reference coincidentally evokes the war in Ukraine. The reference to Ragnorak anticipates mutual assured destruction. This text gestures to the inability of language to fully represent human misery. Echoing Kroetsch, this piece 'effs the ineffable,' baring what happens when words break in our mouths, when communication fails, and when we become lost in the dead-end labyrinths of our minds."

Mobólúwajídìde D. Joseph is a Nigerian writer who lives in Toronto. He recently completed his BA in Communications & Creative Writing at Glendon College, York University, and is currently an MA candidate in Geography at the University of Toronto. His research focuses on homelessness, sur/sousveillance, sociolegal infrastructures, abolition, and community organizing. He is also a Junior Fellow at Massey College.

Joseph writes, "I wrote 'River Boys' for a Black History Month reading at the Harriet Tubman Institute in 2021. I had first encountered the sestina two years earlier in an introductory creative writing workshop, and I found myself returning to the form because of the seeming restrictions it imposes. I hoped the end-word pattern would help scaffold meaning as I worked through the tangled knot of emotions brought on by the reality of being a Nigerian in the diaspora post–George Floyd *and* post-#EndSARS. At the time, I knew I wanted to say something, but I was less sure how to say it. And so, I started with two things: a form, and a place. Water as a central motif feels relevant as a locus of Black healing, vitality, and liberation. In particular, I am reminded of Langston Hughes's 'The Negro Speaks of Rivers,' the Black spiritual 'Wade in the Water,' and Ta-Nehisi Coates's recent marshalling of these traditions in *The Water Dancer*. I was inspired as well by the Biblical referents of Marah and Jordan. I ended up writing it over two months, reading snatches of it out loud to friends, and returning to it again and again. The poem that emerged surprised me both by the scale of its ambition and the fierceness it revealed. In many ways, I am unsure I will be able to write anything like it again."

Penn Kemp of London, Ontario, has been celebrated as a trailblazer since her first publication (Coach House, 1972). She was London's inaugural Poet Laureate and the League of Canadian Poets' Spoken Word Artist (2015). Kemp has long been a keen participant in Canada's cultural life, with over thirty books of poetry, prose, and drama; seven plays and multimedia galore. Recent works include *P.S.* with Sharon Thesen (gapriotpress.com) and *Poems in Response to Peril*. pennkemp.wordpress.com, pennkemp.weebly.com

Kemp writes, "'Cancel Culture' questions itself by returning its title to source. I learnt typesetting by hand with my first book, *Bearing Down*. Fifty years later, that tactile sense lives alongside my love of puns. I'm intrigued by what lives inside a word, as *literate* hides within *obliterate*. In literalizing the metaphor, the poem looks at the long history of a word that casts unconscious shade. What remains, what endures? The etymology of *cancel* offered the notion of cross-hatching as artistic technique and abstraction: intersecting sets of parallel lines. This poem presented itself when I thought cancel culture was at its apex. But no. The boycott of Russian artists is a case in point. (The case, legal, or the wooden box which holds the metal type? Mind can consider many possibilities at once, forefront or subliminal.) In 'What Is the Point of Cancelling Russian Artists?', Katia Grubisic, writing for the *Walrus*, remarks, 'Cultural boycotting as an acceptable collateral consequence of war is egregious. There's no reason to discriminate against individuals.' Egregious but inevitable, when cultural heroes represent their nation. Should they be sanctioned because of their nationality? Should we reclaim shame as a way of decrying public figures when they are, to return to the literal, 'out of line'? Have we lost our ability to laugh at ourselves and other fools, other foolishness? An unfiltered comedian claims, 'I'm just not going to take the piss out of a vulnerable community; I . . . think everyone has one cancellation in them.' (Joanne McNally in the *Guardian*, April 11, 2022.) And then there's celebrity mud-throwing: '#MePoo.'"

Elee Kraljii Gardiner lives in Vancouver, BC, and is originally from Boston. She is the author of two poetry books, *Trauma Head* and *serpentine loop*, and the editor of two anthologies, *Against Death: 35 Essays on Living* and *V6A: Writing from Vancouver's Downtown Eastside*. Her writing has won or been a finalist for the Cogswell Award for Literary Excellence, Raymond Souster Award, bpNichol Chapbook Award, Kroetsch Award for Experimental Poetry, Lina Chartrand Award, Hoffer Award, and the Montaigne Medal. A frequent collaborator, she is also a mentor and director of Vancouver Manuscript Intensive.

Of 'A Mirror of Hieronymous Bosch,' Kraljii Gardiner writes, "I was invited to contribute to an anthology of ekphrastic poems on the paintings of Hieronymus Bosch and fell into a research hole. In my notes for the poem on 'The Temptation of St Anthony' I find this, from Wikipedia: "Smack in the centre of the painting sits a severed foot on a white towel, a representation of ergot poisoning, the result of a fungus in grains, particularly rye seed. Ergotism was epidemic in Bosch's era and persists today on a much lesser scale. The fungus prevents blood flow to the extremities, which in turn causes tissue to rot and blacken. The torturous burning sensations of this process gave ergotism the sobriquets 'hellfire' and 'St. Anthony's Fire'. Other strands of ergotism cause seizures, muscular contractions, delirium and hallucinations, which may have played a role in the behaviour of the girls persecuted in the Salem Witch Trials.' I grew up half an hour away from Salem and always puzzled over what happened there—and I've never understood why people underestimate teenagers. This poem is extremely visual for me, particularly in its use of red and white, but also because of the many memories and locations it mentions. The anthology never came about but I am glad the poem did."

Jeremy Loveday is a poet, arts educator, and city councillor in Victoria, BC, on the territory of the ləkʷəŋən People, known today as the Esquimalt and Songhees Nations. Jeremy is the founder and director of the Victorious Voices youth poetry festival and a three-time Victoria Poetry Slam Grand Champion. In 2020, Jeremy was awarded the Zaccheus Jackson Nyce Memorial Award. His first full-length book of poems is forthcoming from Write Bloody North.

Loveday writes, "I wrote the first draft of 'On Homecoming' in the early days of the pandemic. My partner and I had just moved into a new home, and it was our first time having space to grow our own food and flowers. This practice of cultivation fostered intimacy with the markers of changing seasons and the cycles of death, rot, and rebirth. In challenging and uncertain times, I found grounding and inspiration in the act of planting seeds, turning compost, and feeling my fingers in the dirt. This cultivated numerous reflections on the connectivity between joy and grief, and what it means to act out of hope for the future at a time when human activity has put our planet in peril. 'On Homecoming' attempts to explore these themes while telling the story of Sylvia and her flowers. Many thanks to *Funicular Magazine* for giving this poem its first home."

Randy Lundy is a member of the Barren Lands (Cree) First Nation, in Manitoba. He is the author of four award-winning books of poetry, most recently *Field Notes for the Self* (2020) and *Blackbird Song* (2018). He teaches in the English Department at the University of Toronto Scarborough and is the editor of the Oskana Poetry & Poetics series at University of Regina Press.

Lundy writes, "In the summer of 2019, the MMIWG Final Report was published. Subsequently, a debate occurred in Canadian society about the use of the term *genocide*. Was the term appropriately applied to Indigenous peoples' experiences in Canada? Or not? This is the territory of the poem. There is, in the opening, a reference to critic Theodor Adorno's statement that 'to write poetry after Auschwitz is barbaric,' before a documentation of the staggering number of Indigenous deaths across what is now commonly referred to as *the Americas*. The poem acknowledges the ongoing death and destruction in Indigenous communities as a result of historical and contemporary colonial practice. It links history to the personal, the autobiographical, or what, in poetry circles, is sometimes referred to as the confessional, a mode regularly derided by many among the high-minded. And the poem hears literary editors crying, 'Too didactic!' but chooses to ignore those voices. The assertion is that individual Indigenous people and families bear the scars of colonial practice and a heavy burden of grief, a grief that is communal—this, too, is an intergenerational trauma. In the tradition of Jeannette Armstrong's poem 'History Lesson,' this poem invites Canadians to reflect on the violent history and current realities of this country."

Helen Han Wei Luo is a Chinese-Canadian writer from BC. She is currently a philosophy PhD candidate at Columbia University, where her research centres on the relationship between the moral and the epistemic. Her poetry has appeared in *PRISM international, Sam-Fifty-Four, Cloud Lake Literary,* and *Plenitude Magazine,* and her prose has twice been longlisted for the CBC Literary Prize. She is currently completing a radically feminist novella retelling Han dynasty Chinese mythology, titled *Elegy for Daji.*

Of "Consider the Peony," Luo writes, "This poem opens with a reworked line from Montaigne's *Essays,* on the idea that knowledge belongs to whoever acquires it, no matter its origin: '*the bees plunder the flowers here and there, but afterward they make of them honey, which is all theirs; it is no longer thyme or marjoram.*' It's a profoundly optimistic statement on the power of transformation. Throughout the composition I was compelled by the inverse narrative centred around non-belonging after metamorphosis, particularly around the mythos of immigration stories. There's love here, a violent one—but bitterness too, as the family struggles to reinvent itself after migration. The father rewrites his legacy from nothingness with his son, but loses his daughter. The mother only *almost* runs away with the taxi driver. And of course, the daughter abandons her burden of culture to the bees. I wrote this poem in a rapid and bone-chilling storm of spite—upon revisiting, I'm struck not by the severity, but by the tender sadness. As I see it, the bees never come."

Colin Morton lives in Ottawa with his wife, poet Mary Lee Bragg. His dozen books of poetry include two Archibald Lampman Award winners, as well as *The Hundred Cuts: Sitting Bull and the Major* and *The Merzbook: Kurt Schwitters Poems*. *The Merzbook* also led to a stage play, *The Cabbage of Paradise* (with Jennifer Boyes-Manseau) and the award-winning typewriter animated film *Primiti Too Taa* (with Ed Ackerman). colinmorton.net

Morton writes, "The books I refer to at the start of the poem, by John Cage and Charles Olson, have been on my shelves for decades, and I suppose tinnitus has been with me that long too. It makes one kind of proprioception, sensing the inner workings of the body, unavoidable. The little I have learned about what actually goes on inside the body is amazing, exciting, and also a bit disturbing. Am I one person, an individual, or a host environment for trillions of mites and microbes living lives of their own in or on me? The doctor's advice—'you can complain'—is probably standard. It applies to a lot of things we can't help. In fact, there's a long tradition, a whole genre of poetry devoted to the complaint, as if we poets believe putting the right words in the right order might somehow win back a lost lover, end a war, or give a tinnitus sufferer a moment's peace. For me, getting words in the right order is a matter of listening to the rhythm of the line or sentence forming in my mind and trying to sound out the words that fit. A complaint, however well-spoken, is no cure, but it may give some comfort, or at least pleasure of its own. 'Tinnitus' is a poem I find myself quoting more often than most."

Jordan Mounteer is a visitor on unceded and traditional territories of the Sinixt, Ktunaxa, and Sylix in the Slocan Valley, where he lives and works as a psychotherapist. His poems have appeared in Canadian and American publications, and have won or been shortlisted for a number of awards. He is the author of one book of poetry, *liminal* (SonoNis Press, 2017).

Of "Coyote (*Canis latrans*)," Jordan writes, "This piece belongs to a burgeoning collection of poems centred on 'ecological attention' that so far consists of vignettes or meditations on various taxa—a decidedly sapien attempt at bearing witness. Coyotes (like crows, who earned their own poem in the series) are protagonists who skirt that psychological buffer between non-human and human wildernesses easier than most. That proximity to human consciousness might seem to make them good liaisons when it comes to writing 'nature poems,' but I think it can also show up as a form of dissent. Like, how apparent domesticity, prowling human spaces like roadside gas stations, is less about habituation to humans than a reoccupation of even a quintessentially human experience of loneliness or friendship. And something about that is compelling—a nature poem failing because it has been usurped by its subject?"

Samantha Nock is a Cree-Métis writer from Dawson Creek, BC. Her family is originally from Île-à-la-Crosse, Saskatchewan. She has been published in *Maisonneuve*, *This Magazine*, and *Room Magazine*, amongst others. Samantha currently resides in East Vancouver, on the unceded lands of the Musqueam, Squamish, and Tsleil-Waututh peoples.

Nock writes, "I wrote this piece as a means of longing: longing for the Kiskatinaw, longing for home, longing to be seen fully. I think it can be seen like I am humanizing the river, but I wanted to give agency to her in our relationship. I think common Western views of nature paint it as a passive agent with no autonomy, when in reality, all parts of nature are active in their autonomy and deserve that agency and respect. Ultimately, 'kiskatinaw interlude' is a love poem to a river."

Kathryn Nogue currently lives in Saskatchewan. She is an editor, a writer, and an unaffiliated scholar of Victorian literature and culture. knogue.com or twitter.com/fivefteditrix

Nogue writes, "Being a disabled person in the world means being doubly dehumanized on a regular basis. The medical system is quick to frame one's non-standard body as an aberration in need of fixing. The (temporarily) abled public is often just as quick to reinforce its own sense of normality and superiority by treating that body as an object of disgust, pity, or curiosity. Such ableism isn't a new phenomenon, but it is one people sometimes have trouble acknowledging. 'Thigmomorphogenesis' arose from exhaustion with and an impulse to illuminate the long history of ableism—which includes the freak shows of the late nineteenth/early twentieth centuries and the institutionalization policies of the later twentieth—as well as its costs. The poem suggests the deformative aspect of disability derives not from the condition itself, but the usual reaction to it."

Michelle Porter is a writer and scholar from Alberta. She is the descendant of a long line of Métis storytellers. Many of her ancestors (the Goulet family) told stories using music and today she tells stories using the written word. She is the author of *Approaching Fire, Scratching River,* and a forthcoming novel, *A Grandmother Begins the Story.* Currently, she is teaching creative writing at Memorial University in Newfoundland.

Of "Parts of the Needle, Manitoba, Canada 1870," Porter writes, "This poem speaks about many things all at once, as does our tradition of making clothes. I grew up alongside my mother's sewing machine and her stories of my grandmother and great-grandmother's ability to make beautiful clothes. The sewing machine was alive to me. In a sense I am 'sewing'

Métis history to our people's love of creating beautiful cloth-
ing for themselves and their families. The needle is central to
making clothes, including in beading, of course, but also the
needle on all the old sewing machines that many of our Métis
grandmothers carried with them as far as they could with ev-
ery move. With this poem I am playing with the fact that the
Métis were central to the creation of Manitoba and linking
that to the idea that women's work is also central and also too
often unseen and un-storied. I thread through the poem the
importance of the early Métis leaders, the old way of living
along the Red River, and the provisional government—all of
which are sewn together by a woman's tool, the needle."

Rebekah Rempel lives near Dawson Creek, BC. She studied
creative writing at the University of Victoria. Her poems have
appeared in a number of journals, including *The Fiddlehead,
Prairie Fire, Canthius, Grain Magazine, Room Magazine,* and
Contemporary Verse 2, as well as several anthologies, most
recently *Voicing Suicide* (Ekstasis Editions) and *Sweet Water:
Poems for the Watersheds* (Caitlin Press). One of her poems
received *Canthius*'s 2019 Priscila Uppal Memorial Award for
Poetry.

Of "Potato," Rempel writes, "This poem was initially much
longer. I read an article about different varieties of potatoes
and was inspired by their surprising colours and beautiful
names (content that didn't make it into the final draft, as
sometimes happens). When exploring the subject of potatoes,
it's difficult not to think about the Great Famine, so the poem
wandered there, and eventually to a final stanza that con-
tained the image of roots 'thin and white as an infant's bones.'
When I shared an early draft with my writers' group, two
pieces of feedback had an impact on my revisions. One writer
wondered if the final stanza could stand alone as the poem.
Another writer felt that the poem placed too much blame on
the potato for the Famine, considering that large quantities of
other foods, which could've fed the Irish people, continued to

be exported to Great Britain. With these comments in mind, I cut everything except the final stanza—a stressful decision at first. But it served the poem better. I then wrote many more drafts of this shorter poem, trying to push the meaning further—and more accurately shift the 'blame'—without feeling heavy-handed or didactic. I wanted to avoid a political commentary or history lesson. I knew that the poem had to remain focused on the potato itself, and I had to let the images do the work."

Armand Garnet Ruffo is an Anishinaabe writer from Treaty 9 territory in northern Ontario and a band member of the Chapleau Fox Lake Cree First Nation. A recipient of an Honorary Life Membership Award from the League of Canadian Poets, he is recognized as a major contributor to both contemporary Indigenous literature and Indigenous literary scholarship in Canada. In 2020, he was awarded the Latner Canada Writers' Trust Poetry Prize for a body of work, and, in 2021, a Principal's Teaching and Learning Award from Queen's University. He currently lives in Kingston, Ontario.

Ruffo writes, "My poem 'Observed and Observing, That's Him' came about because the poetry editor of *The Walrus* asked me if I had anything that they could consider for their summer reading issue. I went through my folder, and I didn't have much that I thought would be suitable for them. Poetry books and journals are essentially read by poets, and magazines like *The Walrus* have a much more eclectic readership. I wanted to send them something that would appeal to people who don't generally read poetry. Meanwhile, I had to fix the eaves of my roof because a squirrel was getting in. While I was up on my ladder, there just happened to be a wedding going on in the backyard across the street. This was during the height of the COVID pandemic. Much of what happened is in the poem, but what inspired the writing was considering our differing perspectives. As I was looking down on them, they were looking up at me. I saw them in their finest wedding attire while they saw me in my old work clothes. One of the foundational devices of poetry, though mostly associated with fiction, is perspective or point-of-view. I think it is fundamental to how a creative writer gets from A to B to Z. Once I had this idea fixed as a kind of scaffolding—to use a fitting building metaphor—the poem fell into place."

Richard Sanger grew up in Ottawa and lives in Toronto. He has published three collections and a chapbook, *Fathers at Hockey* (2020). *Dark Woods* was named one of the top ten poetry books of 2018 by *The New York Times*. He also writes essays and plays.

Sanger writes, "The general inspiration for 'Release' must be pretty obvious; the particular legal disclaimer that set this poem going was found on the back of a cross-country ski pass for the Frost Centre trails in the Algonquin Highlands in February 2015. What attracted me was the peculiar legalistic megalomania that seeks to encompass all possible eventualities within the syntax of a single sentence—that need or desire to foresee, name, and contain all the disasters the world may hold in store for us. Maybe poets and lawyers share more than they think. My poem parodies the language, but that doesn't mean the things described don't really happen (viz. real toads, imaginary gardens). Many of my favourite poets—Góngora, Borges, Bishop—are master list-makers and I especially admire the way their best poems can accelerate from the inconsequential to the cosmic and shattering. Thus Bishop's 'One Art' moves from 'my mother's watch' to 'cities' and 'realms,' or Góngora ends a sonnet: *'en tierra, en humo, en polvo, en sombra, en nada.'* 'Load every rift with ore,' Keats told Shelley, which I take also to mean push each poem as far as it can go. Hence the ending. Oh yes, need I add that 'Release' made the rounds and was rejected by at least half a dozen editors? No one seemed to want it and I began to think it wasn't much good until *The New Quarterly* plucked it out of a pile and here it is."

Nedda Sarshar is an Iranian-Canadian writer from the Greater Toronto Area. She is in the process of writing her first short stories series centred on life in the Iranian diaspora, and has had work published in *The New Quarterly, The / temz / Review,* and *PRISM international.* She loves writing about immigrant families, identity crises, and star-crossed lovers.

Of "Why did we bury the ashes?" Sarshar writes, "I have the absolute pleasure of calling Isabella Wang, one of Canada's most prodigious poets, one of my closest friends and it was during a Zoom call where we were discussing poetic forms that she recommended I try my hand at repetition and see where it took me. I was very new to poetry, terrified of its potential, and I don't know what guided me to write about my grandfather's life and passing. It was a good early lesson that risks in art often pay off. At this point Babai had been gone for two years, but the million memories I had of him came at me at random moments every day—glimpses of trying to stay awake while he drove me home from school, playing back-gammon together in the living room, and of course, spending time in his garden—and I needed an outlet to list them and stare at them on the page, and let them be celebrated instead of keeping them caged in my own mind. I'm thrilled that others seem to enjoy the poem as well, for me it's a tender good-bye to someone who I know loved me deeply."

K.R. Segriff is a poet and filmmaker based in Toronto. Her work has appeared in *The Greensboro Review, PRISM international,* and *Prairie Fire* magazines, among others. She is working on her first poetry collection.

Of "The Grannies in Dew Dresses," Segriff writes, "This poem is inspired by my grandmother who considered herself a rebel because she wore slacks. I wrote it after a springtime visit to her grave. Within sight of her plot are those of all of her former euchre buddies and fellow church ladies. I imagined for them an afterlife—complete with insights and enlightenment not possible while they were still in the thick of living—

that mirrored the female companionship I witnessed during their later lives. It is a poem that contemplates the shackles of the postwar existence of rural Canadian women and what they might have grown into had they not been born into that particular set of expectations."

Christina Shah was born in Ottawa, lives in Vancouver, and works in heavy industry. Her poetry has appeared in *The Fiddlehead, Vallum, Arc, Grain, PRISM international, EVENT, The Malahat Review, The Antigonish Review,* and elsewhere. Her poem 'they canned a good man today' was shortlisted for *The Fiddlehead*'s 2021 Ralph Gustafson Poetry Prize. She is one-fifth of the Harbour Centre 5 poetry collective, and has some strong opinions on soft pretzels.

Shah writes, "'interior bar, 1986' is a tribute to British Columbia's resource-economy roots. At the time (among insiders), BC used to be known as the 'Las Vegas of the North,' during an era when dancers used to travel on a circuit of smoky bars, flush with the cash of working men—loggers, fishers, and miners. This poem was also inspired by Vincent van Gogh's painting *Night Café;* he once wrote 'the night is much more alive and richly coloured than the day.' It is a study in contrasts between light and dark, hope and despair, thrill and boredom. The flamboyance of the dancer's costumed appearance and the play of the lights are in contrast to the grimy room and the boozy exhaustion of the patrons. It portrays a woman who dreams of making a better life for herself while navigating the hard living that goes with making it happen. The subjects struggle with isolation and transience, their desire for companionship, and the gulf between men and women in these settings. This is a world of dangerous work (both dancing and underground mining) washed down with booze and drugs, and fuelled by money that is hard-earned and easily spent."

Sandy Shreve lives on BC's Pender Island, where she now spends most of her time painting. She has published and edited or co-edited a dozen books and chapbooks, most recently *In Fine Form: A Contemporary Look at Canadian Form Poetry* (co-edited with Kate Braid, Caitlin, 2016) and *Waiting for the Albatross* (Oolichan, 2015). Sandy founded BC's Poetry in Transit project, which has been featuring BC poets' work on buses and SkyTrain cars since 1996.

Shreve writes, "Once in a while a poem arrives almost fully realized, a gift from who knows where. This has happened to me only a few times, but 'Late' was one of those gifts. One night, after tossing and turning for a while, I hauled myself out of bed and headed to the bathroom. There, I found the most astonishing beauty. Nothing had changed from earlier in the day, or even from the day before. The same towels on the racks, the same housecoats on the door. But for no particular reason, in that instant when I so casually turned on the light, I noticed—and gaped at—the colours, admiring how they just happened to match so well. This simple image became, for me, a metaphor not just for my marriage but for how the ordinary can be extraordinary. 'Late' speaks to how the things we usually assume are insignificant (if we think of them at all) often have something to tell us, if we just take the time to consider them. The title, besides its literal reference to the middle of the night, suggests we might not want to put off paying attention to those little things we tend to ignore. (I should note there were a few edits after the initial writing. The word 'pink' in the first draft was 'pinks.' And the editors at *Exile* astutely noticed a redundant phrase in the fifth line, which, once I happily removed it, called for some line break changes.)"

Adrian Southin is a settler living in the traditional and unceded territories of the Sḵwx̱wú7mesh Úxwumixw (Squamish), səlilwətaʔɬ (Tsleil-Waututh), and xʷməθkʷəy̓əm (Musqueam) Nations. An MFA recipient from the UBC School of Creative Writing, Adrian's poetry and sci-fi explores gender, disability, mental health, and intergenerational trauma. His writing has appeared in *EVENT, Prairie Fire,* and other magazines, and has been shortlisted for several contests including *sub-Terrain*'s Lush Triumphant Prize and *The Malahat Review*'s Open Season Awards.

Southin writes, "'*Dérangement*: Île Saint-Jean' retells the forced displacement of Acadian settlers from Epekwitk through the perspective of my ancestor Louis Longuepée, a man of French and Mi'kmaq heritage. Epekwitk was colonially known as Île Saint-Jean, and now Prince Edward Island. Louis and his family fled to Epekwitk for fear of expulsion, abandoning the village in Wagobagitk/Cobequid (now Colchester County, NS) that bore his name. When British forces later seized the remaining Mi'kmaq territory under French claim (including Epekwitk) in 1758, they began deporting Acadians to France. While Louis's family survived the journey, approximately half of the expelled Acadians died in the Atlantic. He and his children would die in the country colonial powers said they belonged to, yet one to which they had never been. The Acadians remained committed to their homeland, and Louis's grandchildren would eventually return to Epekwitk. Louis's story stands as another example of how colonialism erases identity; his was rooted to the land he grew up and laboured on, not in being a French or English subject. It's been important to me to use Mi'kmaq and French place names not only for inhabiting a historical perspective, but also to acknowledge such erasure. This poem is part of a larger project exploring my family history, and the role of Acadians as both displacers and displaced."

J.J. Steinfeld, a poet, fiction writer and playwright, lives on Prince Edward Island and has published twenty-three books, including *An Unauthorized Biography of Being* (stories, Ekstasis Editions, 2016), *Absurdity, Woe Is Me, Glory Be* (poetry, Guernica Editions, 2017), *A Visit to the Kafka Café* (poetry, Ekstasis Editions, 2018), *Gregor Samsa Was Never in the Beatles* (stories, Ekstasis Editions, 2019), *Morning Bafflement and*

Timeless Puzzlement (poetry, Ekstasis Editions, 2020), *Somewhat Absurd, Somehow Existential* (poetry, Guernica Editions, 2021), and *Acting on the Island* (stories, Pottersfield Press, 2022).

Steinfeld writes, "In my poem 'I Thrust My Left Hand Forward While Thinking of the Past,' I attempt to confront the effects of the Holocaust on subsequent generations generally and on myself specifically as a son of Holocaust survivors, exploring the influences of the past, memory, and history on myself and the surrounding world. This poem attempts to understand how my Jewish identity has been shaped by the Holocaust and what my parents went through during the Second World War and afterward. The thematic approach of 'I Thrust My Left Hand Forward While Thinking of the Past' is a continuation of both the poetry and the fiction explorations in two earlier collections of mine, *Identity Dreams and Memory Sounds* (poetry, Ekstasis Editions, 2014) and *Dancing at the Club Holocaust* (stories, Ragweed Press, 1993). I also have a short fiction version of 'I Thrust My Left Hand Forward While Thinking of the Past,' based on my poem, and included in *An Unauthorized Biography of Being*. When dealing with difficult subject matter, sometimes I approach the ideas and trauma through both poetry and fiction, and on occasion developing those themes through drama."

Sarah Yi-Mei Tsiang lives in Kingston and is the author of ten books, including *Grappling Hook,* her latest from Palimpsest Press. She is currently the poetry editor for *Arc Poetry Magazine* and the creative director of Poetry in Voice.

Tsiang writes, "'Choice' was written right in the thick of things. In early February 2020, at the age of forty-one, I found out that I was unexpectedly pregnant (I already had two children). When I found out I was pregnant I was already juggling multiple jobs and a series of life challenges. At the same time my writing group, the Villanelles, were challenging ourselves to write a poem for every day in February. Though I hadn't planned on writing about the pregnancy (and writing was the last thing I wanted to do), I doggedly tried to write a poem for every day of February. Trying to avoid the subject that obsessed my every waking moment was futile. Even though I wasn't ready to share these very raw and emotional poems with the group, I did report each day that I had written. Though I really didn't want to write at the time, I have to admit that facing that blank page every day helped clarify my life and my choices."

Eric Wang is a writer from Ontario. He is beginning the pursuit of an MFA from the University of British Columbia and has studied at the University of Toronto Scarborough. His poems can be found in *Guernica, PRISM international,* the *New Orleans Review,* and elsewhere.

Of "Poem after Group Text Anticipating Next Millennium's Sushi Date," Wang writes, "This poem, as the title not so subtly notes, is an ode to one of my favourite group chats, to the sadness and love that was shared between distanced friends during the pandemic. Living in quarantine made it necessary for me to recontextualize beauty and where I thought it might be found—in lieu of outside spaces, of close-knit and physically present acts of friendship, of clasping shoulders and holding hands, I instead found my attention drawn to the comfort and wonder in emojis, niche memes, and text-based sushi fantasies. As life ultimately has a way of scattering us all, the sushi date still hasn't happened and, honestly, might not for a few years (yes, I know, not exactly a millennium). Nevertheless, the group chat remains, as well as the beauty I find in it, and in my friends, every day."

Tom Wayman received BC's 2022 George Woodcock Award for Lifetime Achievement in the literary arts. In 2015 he was named a Vancouver, BC Literary Landmark, due to his efforts to foreground writing by people about their daily employment and its effects on them. Since 1973, he has published innumerable books of poetry, fiction, and cultural criticism, most recently *Watching a Man Break a Dog's Back: Poems for a Dark Time* (Harbour, 2020).

Of "Father Pier Giorgio Di Cicco Enters into Heaven," Wayman writes, "I was friends with Giorgio since 1975. I was writer-in-residence at the University of Windsor in 1975–76, and was up to Toronto a lot since my parents lived there. I was impressed by his poems, by his determination to not be Peter George, and by his insistence that poets born in Italy or of Italian descent had a voice that needed to be heard, not least because Toronto's population had become about one-quarter Italian at that point. His appointment as Toronto's Poet Laureate 2004–2009 was a wonderful validation of his beliefs. In wanting to write an elegy for him after his sudden death, I was concerned to achieve the right tone, to be sure the poem reflected his quirky personality and not be about my sense of loss. The poem first appeared in *The New Quarterly*, and I talk in detail on their website about my choice of tone: tnq.ca/finding-the-form-with-tom-wayman/. Giorgio was generous, deeply caring about other people and poetry, convinced that we could fashion better human communities. He was also no respecter of authority—secular or ecclesiastical—and determined to live life (and, presumably, the afterlife) his way. At the same time, Giorgio's friends often found some of his behaviours slightly ridiculous, although Giorgio took our gentle ribbing in good humour. Lindsay's elegy for the founder of the Salvation Army, some lines from which I use as the epigraph, has some of that mix of affectionate mockery and real respect I wanted my poem to capture."

Jan Zwicky grew up in the northwest corner of the Great Central Plain on Treaty 6 territory, and was educated at the universities of Calgary and Toronto. She currently lives on Canada's west coast in a temperate rainforest succession. Human history in the area is complex: the territory is unceded and reflects Coast Salish and Kwakwa̱ka̱'wakw influences. Zwicky is the author of over twenty books of poetry and prose, including *Songs for Relinquishing the Earth, The Long Walk,* and *Wisdom & Metaphor.*

Of "Far from Rome," Zwicky writes: "Northrop Frye said, 'The fact that revision is possible, that the poet makes changes not because [the poet] likes them better but because they *are* better, means that poems . . . are born not made. The poet's task is to deliver the poem in as uninjured a state as possible, and if the poem is alive, it is equally anxious to be rid of [the poet], and screams to be cut loose from [their] private memories and associations, [their] desire for self-expression, [etc.]' ('The Archetypes of Literature,' §VII of My Credo: A Symposium of Critics, *Kenyon Review,* 13.1: 92–110, at 97, my italics). I think Northrop Frye is right, and his account helps us understand why it is a matter of justice and respect to let poems speak for themselves."

NOTABLE POEMS

Mia Anderson
    "Asparagus"
    The New Quarterly 159

Manahil Bandukwala
    "Even at its most difficult"
    The Malahat Review 214

Elena Bentley
    "Learning to Bead"
    The Malahat Review 215

Leanne Boschman
    "Encaustic"
    Grain 48.3

David Bradford
    "Fight Calendar"
    The Fiddlehead 286

Nicholas Bradley
    "Salamandra Salamandra"
    FreeFall 30.1

Andraea Callanan,
    "Asymmetry"
    The Walrus 18.3

Evie Christie
    "Boundary"
    The Walrus 18.1

Rhonda Collis
    "Mary Lake, Muskoka"
    Prairie Fire 42.3

Robert Colman
    "Driving Home from the
    Restaurant, I Forget One
    Word"
    Vallum 18.2

Jan Conn
    "Ironweed"
    The Puritan 52

Kayla Czaga
  "Coho"
  The Walrus 18.8

Dina Del Bucchia
  "Imagine If Celebrities
  Sang 'Imagine'…"
  This Magazine 55.3

Edward Dewar
  "Marionette"
  The New Quarterly 157

Don Domanski
  "A Fox-Shaped Absence"
  The Fiddlehead 286

Arron El Sabrout
  "Body"
  The Fiddlehead 289

Asher Ghaffar
  "From SS Komagata
  Maru"
  Periodicities December
  2021

Elizabeth Gill
  "Oberon"
  The Malahat Review 216

Luke Hathaway
  "As the hart panteth, after
  the water brooks…"
  Arc Poetry Magazine 94

Steven Heighton
  "Familial"
  Vallum 18.1

Shery Alexander Heinis
  "Bloodless"
  Arc Poetry Magazine 96

Matthew [Bettina] Heinz
  "falling forward"
  Arc Poetry Magazine 94

K Ho
  "Recovery Poem"
  PRISM international 60.1

Louisa Howerow,
  After Watching Another
  Military Parade"
  Poetry Pause July 2021

Danny Jacobs
  "The Smoke Eater"
  Hamilton Arts & Letters
  14.1

Rozina Jessa
  "Deep Cove"
  filling Station 77

Jim Johnstone
  "Future Ghost"
  The Fiddlehead 286

Aris Keshav
  "T4T"
  Contemporary Verse 2
  43.3

Judith Krause
  "Advice"
  Grain 49.1

MAGAZINES CONSULTED

Each year, the fifty best poems and the list of notable poems by Canadian poets are selected from more than sixty print and online journals published in the previous year. While direct submissions of individual poems are not accepted, we welcome review copies from print outlets and announcements of new issues from online publications. Please direct two copies of each print issue to Best Canadian Poetry c/o Biblioasis, 1686 Ottawa St., Ste 100, Windsor, ON N8Y 1R1, or email us at bestcanadianpoetry@biblioasis.com.

The Adroit Journal (theadroitjournal.org).
The Ampersand Review. (theampersandreview.ca). Sheridan College, Hazel McCallion Campus, Room B580, 4180 Duke of York Blvd., Mississauga, ON L5B 0G5.
The Antigonish Review (antigonishreview.com). PO Box 5000, Antigonish, NS, B2G 2W5
Arc Poetry Magazine (arcpoetry.ca). PO Box 81060, Ottawa, ON, K1P 1B1
Brick, A Literary Journal (brickmag.com). PO Box 609, Stn. P, Toronto, ON, M5S 2Y4
Bywords (bywords.ca)

Canadian Broadcasting Corporation, CBC Poetry Prize finalists (cbc.ca)

Canadian Notes & Queries (notesandqueries.ca). 1686 Ottawa St., Suite 100, Windsor, ON, N8Y 1R1

Canthius (canthius.com)

The Capilano Review (thecapilanoreview.ca). 102–281 Industrial Ave., Vancouver, BC, V6A 2P2

Carousel (carouselmagazine.ca). UC 274, University of Guelph, Guelph, ON, N1G 2W1

Carte Blanche (carte-blanche.org)

Cascadia Rising Review (cascadiarisingreview.com)

Columba Poetry (columbapoetry.com).

Contemporary Verse 2 (*CV2*) (contemporaryverse2.ca). 502–100 Arthur St., Winnipeg, MB, R3B 1H3

Dalhousie Review (dalhousiereview.dal.ca). Dalhousie University, Halifax, NS, B3H 4R2

EVENT (eventmagazine.ca). PO Box 2503, New Westminster, BC, V3L 5B2

Exile Quarterly (theexilewriters.com). Exile/Excelsior Publishing Inc., 170 Wellington St. W., PO Box 308, Mount Forest, ON, N0G 2L0

Feathertale (feathertale.com/review). PO Box 5023, Ottawa, ON, K2C 3H3

The Fiddlehead (thefiddlehead.ca). Campus House, University of New Brunswick, 11 Garland Ct., PO Box 4400, Fredericton, NB, E3B 5A3

filling Station (fillingstation.ca). PO Box 22135, Bankers Hall, Calgary, AB, T2P 4J5

FreeFall (freefallmagazine.ca). 250 Maunsell Close, NE Calgary, AB T2E 7C2

Funicular Magazine (funicularmagazine.com)

Geist (geist.com). Suite 210, 111 W. Hastings St., Vancouver, BC, V6B 1H4

Grain (grainmagazine.ca). PO Box 3986, Regina, SK, S4P 3R9

HA&L (Hamilton Arts & Letters Magazine) (halmagazine. wordpress.com)

Juniper Poetry (juniperpoetry.com)

The Leaf (brucedalepress.ca). PO Box 2259, Port Elgin, ON, N0H 2C0

The Literary Review of Canada (reviewcanada.ca). 340 King St. E., Toronto, ON, M5A 1K8

long con magazine (longconmag.com)

Maclean's (macleans.ca). 15 Benton Road, Toronto, ON M6M 3G2

Magma Poetry (magmapoetry.com)

Maisonneuve (maisonneuve.org). 1051 boul. Decarie, PO Box 53527, Saint Laurent, QC, H4L 5J9

The Malahat Review (malahatreview.ca). University of Victoria, PO Box 1700, Stn. CSC, Victoria, BC, V8W 2Y2

The Maynard (themaynard.org)

Minola Review (minolareview.ca)

The New Quarterly (tnq.ca). St. Jerome's University, 290 Westmount Rd. N., Waterloo, ON, N2L 3G3

Open Minds Quarterly (openmindsquarterly.com)

Our Times (ourtimes.ca). 407-15 Gervais Dr., Toronto, ON M3C 1Y8

Parentheses (parenthesesjournal.com).

Peach (peachmgzn.com).

perhappened (perhappened.com).

Periodicities (periodicityjournal.blogspot.com).

Plenitude (plenitudemagazine.ca)

Poetry Pause (poets.ca/poetrypause).

Poetry Review (poetrysociety.org.uk/publications-section/the-poetry-review). 22 Betterton Street, London, UK, WC2H 9BX

Prairie Fire (prairiefire.ca). 423–100 Arthur St., Winnipeg, MB, R3B 1H3

PRISM international (prismmagazine.ca). Creative Writing Program, University of British Columbia, Buchanan Room E462, 1866 Main Mall, Vancouver, BC, V6T 1Z1

The Puritan (puritan-magazine.com)

Queen's Quarterly (queensu.ca/quarterly). Queen's University, 144 Barrie St., Kingston, ON, K7L 3N6

Rattle (rattle.com).

Red Alder Review (redalderreview.wordpress.com).

The Rialto (therialto.co.uk/pages).

Ricepaper (ricepapermagazine.ca). PO Box 74174, Hillcrest RPO, Vancouver, BC, V5V 5L8

Riddle Fence (riddlefence.com)

Room (roommagazine.com). PO Box 46160, Stn. D, Vancouver, BC, V6J 5G5

subTerrain (subterrain.ca). PO Box 3008, MPO, Vancouver, BC, V6B 3X5

Taddle Creek (taddlecreekmag.com). PO Box 611, Stn. P, Toronto, ON, M5S 2Y4

Talking About Strawberries (talkingaboutstrawberries.blogspot.com)

The / temz / Review (thetemzreview.com)

This Magazine (this.org). 417–401 Richmond St. W., Toronto, ON, M5V 3A8

Train: a poetry journal. (trainpoetryjournal.blogspot.com)

The Typescript (thetypescript.com)

Understory (understorymagazine.ca). RR#1, Lunenburg, NS, B0J 2C0

untethered. (alwaysuntethered.com)

Vallum (vallummag.com). 5038 Sherbrooke W., PO Box 23077, CP Vendome, Montreal, QC, H4A 1T0

The Walrus (walrusmagazine.com). 411 Richmond St. E., Suite B15, Toronto, ON, M5A 3S5

West End Phoenix (westendphoenix.com). The Gladstone Hotel, 1214 Queen St. W., Toronto, ON, M6J 1J6

Wildness (readwildness.com)

The Windsor Review. (ojs.uwindsor.ca). Department of English, University of Windsor, 401 Sunset Ave., Windsor, ON N9B 3P4

INDEX TO POETS

ACKNOWLEDGEMENTS

"Adjusting the Psychotropics" was originally published in *Myself a Paperclip* © 2021 by Triny Finlay. Reprinted by permission of Goose Lane Editions.

"Alert" appeared in *The Antigonish Review* copyright © Stephanie Bolster. Reprinted with permission of the author.

"Angels: 215>, 1820–1979" appeared in *Poetry Pause/Grain* copyright © Louise Bernice Halfe—Sky Dancer. Reprinted with permission of the author.

"Attention Deficit" appeared in *The Fiddlehead* copyright © Tawahum Bige. Reprinted with permission of the author.

"The Big Dark" appeared in *Prairie Fire* copyright © Patrick Grace. Reprinted with permission of the author.

"Calling It Back to Me" appeared in *The Malahat Review* copyright © Laurie D. Graham. Reprinted with permission of the author.

"Cancel Culture" appeared in *EVENT* copyright © Penn Kemp. Reprinted with permission of the author.

EDITOR BIOGRAPHIES

John Barton is a poet, essayist, editor, and writing mentor. His books include *Polari*; *For the Boy with the Eyes of the Virgin: Selected Poems*; *Seminal: The Anthology of Canada's Gay-Male Poets*; *We Are Not Avatars: Essays, Memoirs, Manifestos*; and *The Essential Douglas LePan*, which won a 2020 eLit Award. Formerly the co-editor of *Arc Poetry Magazine* and editor of *The Malahat Review*, he now lives in Victoria, where he is the fifth poet laureate.

Anita Lahey's latest book is *The Last Goldfish: a True Tale of Friendship* (Biblioasis, 2020). A poet, journalist, essayist, she's also the author of *The Mystery Shopping Cart: Essays on Poetry and Culture* (Palimpsest, 2013), and two Véhicule Press poetry collections: *Spinning Side Kick* and *Out to Dry in Cape Breton*. The latter was shortlisted for the Trillium Book Award for Poetry and the Ottawa Book Award. Anita's magazine journalism has received several National Magazine Award honourable mentions. Anita grew up in Burlington, Ontario; has lived in Toronto, Montreal, Fredericton, and Victoria; and has close family ties to Cape Breton Island. She now lives in Ottawa, on unceded Alongonquin, Anishinabek territory, with her family and their little black cat, Milli.